GABE OPPENHEIM

The Ghost Perfumer

Part I: Creed, Lies, & the Scent of the Century

Solicitude

To Barry and Sara, for affording me a West Coast chamber in which to work (and for tolerating my tack-effectuated punctures of its walls).

And for the brilliant Larry M., whose Santa Monica seafood meals— and the belief in me such occasions signaled— I herewith hope to repay and validate.

Contents

Introduction

At the beginning of 1999, the New York Times insisted the 56-year-old's appearance was still distinguished: He had "the burnish of the Paris Match eurocracy: steely, graying hair, Riviera-toned skin. Prince Rainier by way of Austin Powers."[1]

But very soon, Monsieur Oliver Creed will have crepe-paper skin and a round, jutting chin. His cheeks and forehead won't quite sag – not right away — but they'll seem subject to a slightly greater gravity than the rest of him. Unimpeachably handsome once, he will become a pendulous fellow over the next decade, before becoming fully pot-bellied after yet another.

Now, on the precipice of all that, the start of autumn and the end of a century, September of 1999, Olivier sits in a small boutique north of Houston Street.[2] The shop itself is a fitting setting for a conversation with this particular monied divorcé, who drives a Ferrari and dates a woman 20 years his junior.

The shop abuts the Robbins & Appleton Building at 1-5 Bond, designed by renowned architect Stephen Decatur Hatch in the Second Empire Style – with an iron façade and mansard roof – in 1879 and designated a New York City Landmark exactly 100 years later.

Meanwhile, the building in which the man sits was constructed in 1904 without ingenuity – it was simply built to resemble its neighbor, to the snickering of architectural critics. Creed arrived here from his home in Paris by way of the Concorde.

And so he lounges sipping tea, this middle-aged roué, in fastgentrifying NoHo, pausing to discuss in French, with the help of his New York-based US distributor and publicist, the nature of his work – in particular the nine custom fragrances he crafted the previous year for VIP clients at a cost of anywhere from $10,000-$20,000 each.

"I psychoanalyze the clients," the man says. "We talk about everything. About nothing. If they go to the countryside, what do they do there?"

He must learn about clients' sex lives, his distributor adds.

Olivier says he requires about three or four fittings to get a person's unique scent just so, that he spends 40 hours sniffing each creation as it is made, that each client receives a five-year-supply of bespoke perfume, and that he recently conceived his non-bespoke, commercial fragrance Green Valley while playing golf. And he can really only force himself to work three hours a day.

Also did you know that he skis? "He's very sporty," says the distributor. And he smokes a Cuban cigar every afternoon.

That Olivier is a caricature of a Frenchman born into great wealth – that his definition of sporting would be rather brutally challenged just a few Subway stops away, say in Rucker Park, or just over the Manhattan Bridge, in Gleason's Gym – is obvious. He fits in downtown no better than Crocodile Dundee, if for reasons less outback-tough than Gallic-smug.

Less clear is why this man proclaiming himself a perfumer is being accorded such respect – by the reporter present now from The New York Observer, by the Times journalist who profiled him earlier in 1999, by the New Yorker writer who'll mention Creed in two years' time.

Is that, too, due to money? Or perhaps it's merely due to the family history elucidated on its web site:

"Olivier CREED is the eminent sixth generation master perfumer and chief executive of CREED. Following decades of study of scent with his father, Olivier CREED became master perfumer in 1975. He has created some of the most widely beloved and artistic scents in the 247-year history of the House."

But there is an odd detail included on the press release for this bespoke scent project – namely, that your scent may not be made by Olivier Creed at all but by a perfumer named Jean-Pierre Subrénat, whose career output consists of a co-authored 1978 perfume and three female fragrances for Avon in 1992.

And there is a memoir – a damn entertaining one, in fact – written by Olivier's uncle Charles, a playboy women's couturier of some prominence in the post-war London fashion world who wound up marrying the editor of British Vogue. The book, "Maid to Measure," was published in 1961, or the year Olivier Creed turned 18. It describes a long family history of work in the garment industry but not a word about scent.

Creed shows the reporter a tobacco-based scent of his family's creation that was favored by King George IV, who has been dead, mind you, for 169 years.

"Turkey, Bulgaria, Morocco, southern Italy. Every country has its own smells," Olivier says. "I travel everywhere. Always. La bergamote, le citron, la mandarine! The best is in Sicily. That's where you find good bergamot."

Yeah, sure. The 1961 memoir delves into the life of Olivier's father, too – James Henry, a men's haberdasher with a longtime shop on Rue Royale, that grand avenue leading up to the Luxor Obelisk in Paris. No mention of bergamot.

Perhaps, these are small incongruities – the accounts of the tailors who preceded Olivier versus the family history presented on his firm's web site. Perhaps the inclusion of an additional perfumer in the bespoke scent program's fine-print is owed to some small technicality – that it's no hint of a larger scheme.

That Olivier's lack of any apparent education in the art of aromatic composition, so far as the record shows, was somehow no barrier to his excellence in this realm.

Maybe the flamboyance, the insubstantiality, the sense of entitlement that in nearly every other circumstance would raise a reporter's eyebrows is here nothing more than a sign of authentic old-world aristocracy. Oh, the follies of the nobles.

That The New York Times got it right in 1999: Charles and Diana commissioned scents from Olivier.

That British GQ nailed it three years later: the Creeds made scents for "King George, Madonna, Winston Churchill, both Elvises – Presley and Costello – Queen Victoria and Michael Jackson."

Nor was there a mistake in The Independent on Sunday in 2013: Olivier and his forebears had won over customers from "Winston Churchill to Michelle Obama, Frank Sinatra to the Queen."

That when Olivier's son Erwin told The International Herald Tribune in 2004, regarding its VIP clients: "It is how we do things now — not to divulge too much," he was somehow not misrepresenting the company's practice of listing every star customer in its literature, including Natalie Wood, for whom a scent called Jasmal was said to be created in 1959, despite its dating by a historian to 1999, 18 years after the actress' death.

Because for all these claims to be false — for hundreds, if not thousands, of newspaper and magazine articles and profiles – in the most fact-checked of periodicals – to be untrue – Olivier Creed must have perpetrated the greatest fraud in the history of luxury retail.

As this very book was being written, in February 2020, Oliver Creed sold his business to a private capital fund at BlackRock, the largest asset manager in the world, a firm that oversees $8.67 trillion in assets. It was the fund's *first* investment in a European company.

The terms of the deal were not disclosed – nor Creed's books, as the perfumery is private. However, analysts pegged Creed's annual revenue at $200 million (with huge double digit profit margins; the French newspaper Les Echoes estimated it was even higher – $270 million), and the brand's former US distributor told me BlackRock likely paid close to $1 billion.[3]

A financial heavyweight, eschewing oodles of other possible deals, paid a tiny French fragrance operation a billion dollars? This would have to be one preposterously successful perfumery. A grooming brand gone filthy rich.

Which would make the actual creator of the scents – Olivier Creed's Cyrano – the most abused artist in the industry ever.

The press release announcing the deal said BlackRock had valued Creed for its "unique proposition" as a "founder-led" enterprise. The new Creed chairman, the former CEO of Bacardí, added, "The quality of the products that Olivier and Erwin have developed has enabled Creed to become the world's leading artisan fragrance."

Est-ce possible?

* * *

What if I told you that F. Scott Fitzgerald didn't author "The Great Gatsby" — that despite the attribution on the book's cover, the writer's own paperwork and reportage on the project in every major periodical for nearly 100 years – the byline was an incredible hoax? That Fitzgerald, far from penning "Gatsby," had actually paid off a genius colleague with low self-esteem to sell him the manuscript and the right to call it his own? And not only "Gatsby," mind you, but his every other notable work – "This Side of Paradise," "Tender is the Night," all those short stories?

And what if that insecure colleague with daddy issues he'd bought off was none other than Hemingway – so that a proper revision of

Ernest's bibliography now included not just "The Sun Also Rises" and "A Farewell to Arms" and "For Whom the Bell Tolls" but nearly every word ever ostensibly penned by Fitzy?

Such a discovery would shock not just the literary world but anyone who'd ever taken high school English. Moreover, it'd spur a reassessment of Hemingway that would strain the best critics' capacity to evaluate a man – if you've already called Papa the best, if you long ago doled out every superlative, what additional praise could be offered now?

What is infinity plus one?

But of course, this is a silly exercise in alternate history, a flight of sci-fi fancy, you're thinking – we aren't going to find out Fitzgerald was a fraud who purchased his prestige in the manner of Gatsby himself. Nor are we ever to make a similar discovery in another field. These seem almost conspiracy theories, inappropriate even to propose hypothetically in an age of rampant untruth.

But what if there was a field in which this actually did occur – for decades? What if the man who'd bought off the masterpieces had been so successful consequently he'd been able to sell over his supposed life's work to a private equity fund for untold millions?

What if the genius who'd pawned off masterpieces, filled with regret, had retreated to a 19th-century castle in a remote piece of country along a river, refusing to discuss his known career – already lauded – let alone that secret portion of his life's work about which nobody had ever known to inquire?

What if the truth, so bitterly swallowed up, seemed bound to be buried alongside the legend – until a zealous outsider came knocking?

Is that an artistic field in which you might be interested?

Because it happened in perfumery – a Hemingway invented a Fitzgerald.

Welcome to the heady world of fragrance.

* * *

Admittedly, perfumery isn't the domain of a single, striking secret – it's rife with fraudulence.

There are clones whose outrageous pricing makes an implicit claim for originality. There are perfumers who go by multiple names so their output doesn't seem inartistically rapid.

There is rampant philandering – name a great male perfumer of the last century and I will point out his mistress (some of whom became second wives).

But if the perfume world is full of secrets, the following is its greatest:

That the seminal works of the Creed fragrance company were composed not by venal namesake Olivier Creed or his ancestors, as the man and company claim, but by the genius perfumer Pierre Bourdon, whose sense of self-worth, dented by his own father, led him to give up brilliant compositions to Creed for a pittance and thus cover up his role as the primary olfactive artist of his generation.

This is the story of an odorant heist.

Olivier Creed in his US distributor's shop in SoHo, Manhattan, 20 years ago. (Courtesy of Fred R. Conrad/The New York Times/Redux)

Chapter 1: What Is Perfume?

As the best defense is sometimes offense – a sortie in advance of possible objections (to this topic or *my* tackling it).

So you think perfume is not akin to sport or literature? Fair – there are vast differences. But if the composition of original work is always some balance between creative impulse and market consideration, perfumery is most certainly a sufficiently similar endeavor.

Beyond which, what counts as art and sport is a highly cultural determination. In fair France, where we lay our scene (primarily), perfumery has most certainly been treated as a kind of art for centuries. There is a well-regarded French book written about Marie Antoinette's perfumer. There is a university dedicated to fragrance history and creation – *Institut supérieur international du parfum, de la cosmétique et de l'aromatique alimentaire*, more commonly and easily called ISIPCA.

That school's original Versailles campus (it now has a Paris branch as well) is the home of the Osmothèque, a museum that in carefully calibrated climatic conditions preserves samples of the most historically and artistically significant perfumes ever produced.

And then there's my personal reflection, if you'll spare a moment:

Perfumes seem delicious despite being inedible. They are physical fluids that impel abstract thought – evoking monochromatic hues, wilder colors, images. They bookmark moments in time, despite being dissipated by the very same.

Perfume is a lover always in the process of leaving.

A good fragrance is addictive for a chemical reason or simply for the complexity of its unfolding over time. A great one has both qualities and something extra besides – or neither, by daring intention.

A perfumer interprets the present, so as to stimulate a particular future.

We, the users, aromatic enthusiasts, may have turned to fragrances not for the purposes of seduction. But instead out of loneliness, heartbreak, physical pain (I know a small something about the first two and a great deal more about the third). We became reliant then on the flood of feel-good neurotransmitters attendant to our every depression of the atomizer. Next we required darker, deeper, more complex creations to obtain that rush – ever more sniffs of the new and exotic, though we'd settle in desperate moments for the bottles locked behind Plexiglas at CVS.

How addiction takes old.

I favor leather scents – Hermes Bel Ami, Tom Ford Tuscan Leather, By Kilian Royal Leather, Chanel Cuir de Russie, Dior Cuir Cannage, Knize Ten, Memo Irish Leather.

Leather – a pebbled texture – considered richer for having been broken-in by time. Better for the beating it has taken.

Oud – the tarry resin of fungus-infected agarwood: They sit on the floor hacking logs, mad dentists with machetes, prizing perversely the cavity, gooeyness, that which sticks.

Later the scalpel: rows of hunched, barefoot, men, meager and single-minded, carving that which is fragrant from that which is not. Bringing forth facets, polishing edges.

Like the warehoused women of Gujarat, who, working away at rough rocks, erase unwanted layers from what we later call diamonds.

Perfume, too, is a jagged, wild thing — before we call it by that name.

Workers at Ajmal, in Dubai, knifing away oud chips.

A curator of films for an indie movie theater in downtown NYC with whom I once spent an evening in a small Brooklyn apartment with frost-covered skylights and myriad hanging plants, said to me – rather profoundly, I thought – that while perfume can transport you to the era in which you first wore it, it won't do so if you've never stopped using it. Time travel only works if you ceased anointing yourself in the stuff – if you've let it go or it has been taken from you. Scent cannot revive the past if it's intermingled in your mind with the present.

Perfume's magic is inextricably linked to loss.

Isn't that what underlies so much of our activity in the first place – a grasping in the outside world for that which we can only feel within?

* * *

My parents have never been great lovers of aromas, natural or man-made.

Once, on a drive to a NASCAR race in the Poconos, my father discarded the sardine sandwich I had packed in tin foil for lunch because he despised the odor. My mother nearly kicked me out of the house during the ongoing corona quarantine when too many perfume samples arrived in the mail (ostensible signs of my profligacy at a time of serious economic turmoil).

And also because she could catch whiffs of the scents I was trying on in my room, and these air droplets absolutely repulsed her, not because I have bad taste in fragrance or even as a result of experimentation with, say, a potent, fecal natural ingredient such as oud, but because she has never tolerated fine fragrance at all.

When she started dating my father, he had to quit wearing scents entirely. The green Paco Rabanne pour Homme splash bottle he was then using, still in his medicine cabinet today, has been essentially undisturbed for more than three decades (paused mid-usage as if struck by Vesuvius-esque eruption).

I say almost undisturbed because I made use of it once, and only once, in my childhood, when I declined the offer of latex gloves during a school science dissection of owl-emitted rat pellets. My skin's subsequent smell was so horrid and long-lasting, so impervious to soap and scrubbing, I resorted to washing my hands in the Paco juice (and thereafter sealing the smell with the lotion that accompanied the eau de toilette) for a full week. Which resulted in my hands smelling not cleansed but foul and refined in alternate emissions.

* * *

Having spent the majority of my university years and then my 20s covering boxing, I was often asked by interviewees, with no small degree of suspicion, what a fight writer was doing in such a remote realm. That is, in their own.

Perfumers are incredibly territorial – they've no choice, given how few positions exist, how often their best efforts fall short, how eager multinational corporations are to cut them in order to sign promising young prospects.

In this way, in fact, perfumery is akin to contemporary sport: a job is never guaranteed, and you're only as good as your last outing. The elderly and wise are nodded at with ceremony but rarely heeded, if they're lucky enough to have been given some emeritus position from which to observe their boastful successors in the first place.

But this was not my usual answer to perfumers and their company-appointed media handlers when interrogated. Often, I stammered something to the effect that both fragrance and sport are competitive fields and told a few true stories about my wearing certain colognes while reporting on pugs.

This began in 2016, after running with middleweight champ Canelo Alvarez at dawn, just outside San Diego, on the grounds of a horse stable, for a Vice piece. Afterward, huffing in the mansion I'd partly rented via AirBnb, I applied Montblanc Legend so I might present myself for the interview portion of our encounter that afternoon impressively fragrant for a man who'd just far exceeded his body's normal capacity for aerobic exercise.

I've no idea whether this move backfired on me or was unapparent altogether – Canelo, acting like a petulant and spoiled child, refusing to answer the only questions that really mattered, never commented on the role of my aroma in his extended distemper.

Five years later, in 2021, I do think I've the answer about Venn diagram overlap between sanctioned dude-socking events and scent:

Since the inception of both boxing and perfumery (and perhaps fashion and clubbing could be added here, although I've not done the legwork on those) people have been pronouncing these fields dead. And not just anyone, either, but those stakeholders who should be the most educated on their pasts and futures.

Every boxing *macher* complains about the proliferation of titles, the meaninglessness of rankings, the influence of the mob. Even those managers who are in the mob. And: Everyone is a champion so nobody is. The fragmentation of the media covering fights in the first place means no one can quite identify who's on top.[4]

In perfumery, it is all about the proliferation of flankers – that is, scents released yearly with slightly altered names and formulae such that consumers have no idea whether a new release is actually that, whether its alteration was significant enough to make it worthy of new consideration. Every release is the latest olfactory champ so none of them is.

Oh, and America – especially American men. They've stopped watching boxing – they don't care about it as a sport anymore. And they've stopped wearing perfume, haven't been buying bottles for three decades now, and the women are following them, and the death of the department store is only going to hasten the decline. As the end of cable TV dominance has dented the ratings for boxing and made it that much harder to find, let alone watch semi-somnolently.

Except, of course, none of it's true. Boxing wasn't dead when it was claimed to be in the 1960s or centuries ago or now and as for fragrance, men's perfume was called moribund before it ever began to be sold in America in earnest.

In October of 1933, the general manager of couturier Jean Patou, having traveled from France to the US via ocean liner, made his expert pronouncement that American men, if presented with fragrance, "probably would never capitulate" and don it, per The New York

Times,[5] in an article headlined, "Men's Perfume Fashion Gets No Foothold Here." Within five years, the Shulton Company had launched Old Spice. Thirty years from the Patou pronouncement, Shulton's 1963 net earnings were $4.9 million on $71 million of sales.[6] Just to repeat: $71 million effing dollars.

In reality, neither field has ever passed away and neither seemingly will. Nothing dies in the 21st century. The upside of a world on the brink of constant disaster due to societal fracture are small pockets of like-minded people able to keep nearly anything near to their hearts alive. So alive perhaps that to them, connected by technologies that don't turn off, the idea of their being passe is nonsensical, goes against the grain of what they see and feel, however virtually.

There will always be fight junkies and fragheads. They're more connected to each other, and more alone otherwise, than ever – meaning, they're more co-dependent, bonded together more deeply by the mutuality of their passions.

It's the perfumers who are the misunderstanding cynics. Dominique Ropion of IFF can't bring himself to wear a perfume any more layered or complex than a simple citric cologne, despite his constant creation of chemically clever and dynamic scents (more on him to come – what a kind man, never mind that on this issue I've taken him to task).

Fabrice Pellegrin of Firmenich wears ambroxan alone as a perfume — just a single ingredient instead of a composition (Fabrice is also poetic and sweet and the creator of a gorgeous Kilian leather frag).

Yes, it speaks to an understanding of fragrance and perhaps its nature as work to perfumers. But such aromatic asceticism also seems apologetic, as if the creators are saying, almost cravenly:

We know our work perturbs your noses. We promise not to do so on our own time but only to make a living.

* * *

Drops of rain on wood, brick or tin – sounds that makes it safe for us to be silent. Pelting, pinging, puddling — the thrum is a blanket.

Perfume can be the same.

* * *

Fragrance interacts with everything – the tragic and the triumphant; the sublime and the farcical. It trails, wafts, hangs. Precedes us and lives on far after we've gone.

The New York Times, reporting on the discovery of King Tut's tomb in 1923, ran this memorable headline: "PHARAOH'S VASES GIVE OFF OLD SCENT: Tutankhamen's Perfume Still Strong, but Not as Sweet as 3,300 Years Ago."

The article then relayed the following episode: the tomb's discoverer Howard Carter spent two hours in the "broiling" heat removing five alabaster vessels of perfumed unguents (these were later said to be mixtures of incense and coconut oil) before a crowd of female tourists keen on smelling each one.

On the removal of the final jar, "when Mr. Carter told the ladies it was the last for today, they expressed disappointment.

"'What!' said Mr. Carter; 'you have seen five unique treasures in two hours. Isn't it enough?'

In 1967, an 18-year-old US Army soldier in Vietnam named Ralph Del Vecchio and a fellow GI were ordered to place 80 American corpses into bags, in a macabre duty dehumanizingly called "Graves Registration." Their superiors gave them masks soaked in Aqua Velva to cover up the stench.[7]

The significance here isn't so much the insatiable curiosity of 20th-century humans to find out what an ancient perfume smelled like (some mixture of coconut oil and spikenard, apparently) – nor the way scent can be seared in the memory for horrific reasons, its role as adornment perverted.

It's the fact that, while the reader might have perhaps never considered this, both offerings were no mere offshoots of nature – the fragrance of a flower or of the sea, effulgent without human intervention.

These were the works of people.

There was an actual perfumer who composed the scents of King Tut, though his name escapes us. The composer of Aqua Velva of 1935 is identifiable – it was Elmer Sulik of the New York-based company International Flavors and Fragrances, whose star perfumers would go on to make fragrances for Estee Lauder, Ralph Lauren and Halston, these new age alchemists both technically polished and vastly imaginative.[8]

And then there are the perfumers who followed Sulik, at his firm and others, whose works were derivative. Whose methodology involved more market research than creative brainstorming.

Which brings us back to perfumery as literary lion club or sports hall of fame – a realm of striving ripe for comparisons. Are these inevitably subjective judgments? Of course. Does Dickens better capture 19th century London than Zola does Paris? Was the Griffey uppercut the sweetest-looking lefty swing or was the Babe Ruth weight-transfer more beautiful for that pudgy near-free-fall lean?

These are fun arguments to stage – to a point – precisely because there is no definitive answer. Commence the 92nd Street Y panel or sports radio shout show.

Perfume criticism, no less open-ended, is a younger pastime, having commenced in recent years with the publication in 1992 of biophysicist Luca Turin's brilliant evaluation of scents and their makers, *"Parfums le guide."*

I like polymathic Luca a whole lot – not least because he doesn't read books on perfume nor do we engage in comparisons of the perfumers in our correspondence, instead proffering lists and photos of our favorite Italian supercar designs of decades past. We admire edges and curves like giddy boys – kindgarteners high on Countaches.

But at the end of the day, the premise underlying our every exchange, his books, those ESPN argument hours is simply this: We may be unable to rank designs definitively, but at the very least, we have the facts of the developments. How and by whose hand achievement came to be.

These truths matter. Our agreement upon them is the basis for all disquisition thereafter. Bless newspapers for still running corrections.

Here are those of the fragrance industry, then, with no apologies to draftsman-of-doorstops Jonathan Franzen. Prepare to forget everything you ever knew, which was likely little to begin with. Or the tale of how Fitzgerald bought off some of Hemingway's very best work.

Chapter 2: How Perfumery Works

H ow does this industry operate, soup to nuts?

There are a handful of fragrance-formulating companies, such as Firmenich and Givaudan, both Swiss-based and founded in 1895, that employ perfumers, the majority of whom are French. These perfumers formulate new scents but only so that the company can then provide the raw materials for the fragrance to its commissioning vendor. The formulas are dangled bait, in a sense.

These aforementioned vendors are beauty companies that have amassed licenses to create perfume under well-known brand names, mostly those of fashion designers.

Estee Lauder has the rights to Tom Ford, Ermenegildo Zegna and Tommy Hilfiger. L'Oréal has Armani, Ralph Lauren and Yves Saint Laurent. Shiseido has Issey Miyake, Dolce & Gabbana and Narciso Rodriguez. Other prominent licensees include American firm Coty, Puig of Catalonia, Spain, and Inter Parfums, which has a motley array including Coach, Dunhill and Abercrombie & Fitch.

If any firm – say, Estee Lauder, on behalf of Tom Ford – wants a new fragrance, it sends out a "brief" to Givaudan and Firmenich, along with some of their major competitors: Symrise of Germany and International Flavors and Fragrances of New York (smaller firms that also receive briefs, but less often and for less prestigious assignments on the whole: Mane, Takasago and Robertet).

The brief is a minimalist description of the scent desired – a high school essay prompt – which might be a place, a color, a concept thinner than cellophane, although they've become less abstract and more grounded in recent years.

In 1969, Rochas (most of whose scents were made by IFF) put out a brief for a scent that evokes a "cold pipe." The brief for what became Yves Saint-Laurent Opium in 1977 – a lush-spicy oriental – called for "the perfume of a whore," which would mate the formula of Estee lauder's 1953 Youth-Dew (also made by IFF) with more traditional French raw materials.[9]

In 2000, Dior – one of the few designers that choose to make scents in-house, without licensing its name – requested a scent "as sexy as a stiletto and as comfortable as a pair of Tod's." This became megahit J'Adore Dior – you might have seen its bottle like a golden bowling pin or its advertising featuring Charlize Theron.

J'Adore is also a lesson in the meaningless of the prompt – or, rather, the degree to which a fragrance marketer speaks a language different from that of its petitioned creator. Dior mentioned shoes in its brief, but the winning composition by Calice Becker – then of Quest, which would later be bought by Givaudan – was based in part on her grandmother's recipe for a plum compote with Banyuls wine.

Current briefs are far more likely to mention other scents with enviable characteristics – in other words, to ask for a "twist," in industry parlance, on a current market hit, as YSL once did when creating Opium based on Youth-Dew. If that sounds like rank unoriginality, it is – but originality is scarcely prized in contemporary fragrance. The brief for Armani Acqua di Gio, of 1996, was all about a physical location in Sicily. The brief for Polo Blue of 2002 was: Mr. Ralph Lauren wants *his* Acqua di Gio.

Moreover, the number of firms briefed determines the diversity of entries – but Firmenich and Givaudan and IFF and Coty and Symrise only send briefs to perfume companies on their "core lists." That is, they purposely don't brief every perfumer (despite that detrimental effect on creativity). Their stated reason is that briefing everyone would require them to spend an inordinate amount of time reviewing entries.

Some additional work would be necessary, but the real reason for core lists, which are revised every 3-4 years, is so Lauder, L'Oréal, Coty and their ilk can shake down the perfume makers – Givaudan, Firmenich, IFF, Symrise – which offer incentives and rebates to secure these lucrative spots on the core lists.

"Every four years or five years, they are asking for more money," a perfumer told me. "It's becoming indecent."

Yes, that's right – perfume firms pay to compete merely for the chance to make a scent. One form these pricing breaks take is pre-negotiated margins on raw materials, which are alternately known as "the oil." Remember: a perfumer's brief-winning formula is not what makes a Givaudan big money but the commitment of a Lauder to buy the raw materials for the realization of this formula from Givaudan for the duration of the perfume's market life (some scents aren't discontinued for decades). So a pre-negotiated margin means no matter how popular the perfume, a Givaudan cannot capitalize by charging more for the goods.

But that's still indirect pay-to-play. One perfumer told me a non-French, non-Swiss fragrance firm, which did a lot of business in functional fragrance a few years ago – think detergent — and little in fine fragrance, was for that reason so desperate to boost its perfumery operations in the eyes of analysts it paid Coty three times the going shakedown rate to claw its way onto the Coty list.

"If someone can explain the difference between this and extortion

I'd be most grateful," a highly-regarded perfume expert told me.

As of this writing in late 2020, IFF, despite having produced bestseller Axe Dark Temptations, is no longer on Unilever's core list for Axe briefings. This has IFF executives working overtime now to assemble a package lavish enough to satisfy Unilever.

Similarly, a recent redo of Estee Lauder's Core List saw Givaudan win the near-exclusive right to work on Tom Ford scents despite Firmenich having produced some of the brand's greatest hits (Grey Vetiver, Tuscan Leather, Noir de Noir) – although Firmenich did retain the right to be briefed on certain significant Tom Ford projects (because even when your money doesn't talk, it can still whisper; and as far as Lauder is concerned, too much is never enough).

* * *

Perfumes are lately treated as open-code software – their elements divined by deformulation, or reverse-engineering, via gas chromatograph. In layman's terms, all perfumers are college students taking a final exam not only afforded the opportunity to peer at their neighbors' blue books but by the proctors handed said essays.

The GC machine itself takes in juice and spits out cloudy puffs; the identity of each puff is an ingredient in formula being broken down. There are literally techs at oil houses whose job is simply to submit every new fragrance on the market to a GC analysis and upload the results – the nominally secret formula — to the company's computers.

Perfumers literally have at their fingertips access to the chemical tricks of everyone in the trade. Their offices abound in cheat sheets. The question then becomes not whether to access such information but how to make use of it – as the basis for a scent related conceptually but compositionally novel – or for a straight-up clone – a one-to-one copy of the juice made by a competitor – which is legal, amazingly, though it'd be the stuff of plagiarism suits in any other creative industry (yo, Coldplay – to my ears, you stole "Viva La Vida" from Joe Satriani, and I imagine your private settlement out of court compensated him accordingly).

Actually, there is *one* element of intellectual property protection in perfume: The oil houses – Givaudan, Firmenich, IFF...etc. – hold patents on certain molecules they create themselves, for 4-15 years, called "captives." These cannot be duplicated, though they can sometimes be closely mimicked.

A perfumer can check up on his company's latest materials – or another's unprotected ones – in a database, which covers each ingredient's characteristic scent, tenacity on a paper smelling strip (could be anywhere from one hour to one month), and advisable concentrations for its usage in perfume, candles, shower gels and cleaning products.

Software is also instrumental in the formulation of scents – although not in the ways industry execs once promised in TED Talk future-speak – that machine learning of historical fragrance composition plus the aforementioned chemical databases could enable AI to suggest felicitous pairings of raw materials human perfumers might never devise.

Yes, the German firm Symrise has a deal with IBM to use its Watson software for this ostensible purpose, but it doesn't really save for a publicity project now and again, nor does any of the firms yet utilize such a scarily HAL-esque level of digital intervention.

Instead, computers serve what seems far more prosaic purposes daily: first, when a perfumer sends a new mod (as in formula modification) into the company lab, whereas technicians and assistants would formerly compound that formula for spraying and testing purpose entirely manually, now a robot can do up to 50 percent of the weighing of the raw materials itself (so when that system goes down, even the snootiest of perfumers might be forced into the lab to do some hardscrabble measuring); second, as licensees set budgets on how much all the oil in a formula can cost per kilo, all the raw material houses have spreadsheet software that balances the budgets for a perfumer.

Take away from the amount of rose absolute and your budget to increase the usage of Indonesian patchouli oil is tabulated accordingly. This is no minor help – without such software, a perfumer would have to keep constant tabs on the precise cost of raw ingredients and constantly re-multiply the numbers with each slight shift in the complementary balance of materials.

Givaudan is now switching over from its old tabulation software – called The Sphinx – to its new one – called iSphinx. So yeah, that's about how far along computers have come in the perfume sphere – yes, they enable the pricing of molecules and the peering at competitors' compositions, but they're also somehow only just arriving to that Jobs-ian notion that all things electronic must begin with an "i."

Well, almost. Givaudan has recently faced the very same social media problem we all have: the proliferation of hurtful comments made merely for sport or the achievement of a perverse popularity—and the resultant obscuring of potentially useful, constructively-critical discourse.

Not wanting its perfumers to examine the unedited awfulness — to delve deeply into the cesspool of cruel commentary — Givaudan's top bosses now use a software program (potentially one engaged in machine-learning, though I couldn't confirm that) that extracts only *helpful* consumer responses from the web and supplies them to the scentmakers.

Did several perfumers admit checking the web for public feedback on their work anyway? Of course. They are very human — no matter how high-minded their bosses are in trying to shield 'em.

* * *

Once a brief is received, the firm's perfumers begin looking over their favorite accords – blends of notes that give the impression of a larger element, say, leather – and figuring which to submit. This means colleagues within a company are at war not just with rival firms' hands but also each other.

Ultimately, a few entries pass the first round, their crafters told by the licensee to make adjustments. It could be a more citric top note or a darker base. Anywhere from a few to a hundred assays follow before a product is accepted, the entries pared down to just one or two along the way. L'Oréal requests the most mods, generally – Yves Saint Laurent Libre went through 1,000 different alterations before being okayed for market (my high school girlfriend and forever-bestie, whose nose I will rely on often in these pages, found it horrid in spite of those refinements – or perhaps because of them).

The process isn't quite the same at every licensee. L'Oréal, further, doesn't immediately have its top fragrance guru rate entries. Rather, these submissions go to a "cellule olfactive" or "olfactive thinktank" – a group of highly-opinionated evaluators. One particular member, Karine Lebret Leroux, is especially polarizing, alternately admired for a keen nose by some and despised for an unlettered perspective by others.

One perfumer, formerly of Givaudan and Takasago and now independent, told me the hugely successful Armani Code only made it to the market because Lebret was mercifully on maternity leave then and unable to offer input.

A current Givaudan perfumer's rebuttal: "She's a tough cookie. But I find her brilliant."

But the most unique aspect of L'Oréal's process isn't the olfactive cell's feedback – it's the company's practice of soliciting scents not for a single fragrance but for their licensed brands' general future use. In this way, the perfumers have no idea sometimes whether they are working on an Armani, YSL or Ralph Lauren – whatever they're told one day may be contradicted the next.

A perfume is sometimes shifted between brands for nebulous reasons for years prior to its release – and when it's thusly held up in purgatory, a perfume is said to be in L'Oréal's *"panier,"* or basket.

A 2021 masculine from L'Oréal started life in 2016 as a scent designated for Diesel and became a Puma scent and then a Diesel again before finally reaching the market as an Azzaro – a brand whose license L'Oréal hadn't even possessed when the perfume was first created.

Now, the scent's success hinges in part on the reputation of a brand to which it had no intrinsic connection during the vast majority of its half-decade gestation.

Still, a perfumer can console herself that no matter the cold, almost disinterested way L'Oréal treats her submissions, dealing them to brands like a croupier does cards, at least those involved in the process have some olfactive training.

Amazingly, that isn't the case at Inter Parfums – the lamely-named licensee of Abercrombie & Fitch, Coach and Montblanc – which asks distributors of its products around the world which perfumer submissions would sell in their regions and which wouldn't. A perfumer's submission can then be eliminated from the competition – no matter its merit – based on a salesperson's doubts.

Yes, that does strike perfumers as an affront, and it forces even the most genuine among them to design scents for Inter Parfums cynically, to condescend to the mindset of wannabe wheeler-dealers – folks straight off the set of "Glengarry Glen Ross," posted across the world.

But there are also far more lettered lightning rod figures – which is only natural. How could gatekeepers – those who decide which entries reach production, despite not having attained the rank of perfumer, in the first place – prove anything but controversial? Their job is to gather a mob of perfumers only to tell nearly all of 'em "not quite, no" and one person (or team) "yes."

Ann Gottlieb, a former Lauder employee who boldly established her own consulting firm, became the feared and revered evaluator for Calvin Klein during its musky, unisex '90s heyday, as well as the gatekeeper for Axe, Carolina Herrera and Marc Jacobs. If your juice didn't please her, it would never see the inside of a bottle.

There's a PBS documentary from 1995 in which Gottlieb can be seen forcefully requesting perfumer Sophia Grojsman of IFF to redo her work over the weekend so a new version can be ready by Monday. The language is sharp and direct, devoid of sentimentality. There's the presumption that Sophia had no plans over the weekend and even if she had, she'd cancel them, no problem. Of course, Sophia agreed to get the work done in time.

A viewer would never guess that Grojsman was considered the best deviser of women's scents just a few years earlier or that this tremendous reputation was earned in part for her creation of Calvin Klein Eternity – a juice made under aegis of the very same tough-love overseer ordering her about in the present – none other than Ann Gottlieb.

At Lauder, Estee's personal protégée, Karyn Khoury, long held sway. Her tight relationship with Tom Ford himself — her ingenious divining of what he wanted and which submissions would please him – made her almost singlehandedly responsible for the brand's epochal entry into the cosmetics sphere in 2007.

It's hard to exaggerate how important the Tom Ford scents have been in the market. For instance, following the release of Tuscan Leather of 2007, nearly every other market leather has either mimicked that standard or slyly eluded its raspberry-petrol signature.

Khoury's role in this scent's development is instructive: At Firmenich, Harry Fremont had for years toyed with a leather accord reliant on isobutyl quinoline, a chemical commonly used in leathery composition. Khoury decided this wasn't quite enough to make the aroma distinctive and had the accord combined with a raspberry concoction devised by another Firmenich hand, Jacques Cavallier. A simple addition, sure, but one that sprang from a quick, supple mind and no small amount of gumption: You try telling two perfumers working on unalike projects to literally combine their work...and have the result come out both divine and bombastic.[10]

Perhaps no less bold has been the way Khoury and Ford in tandem have attempted to take advantage of American olfactory ignorance and amnesia. Along with the genuinely new scents they've solicited from the briefed perfumers at Givaudan and Firmenich, they've also issued under the Tom Ford name thinly veiled versions of classic scents.

Tom Ford Noir is a retread of Guerlain Habit Rouge, first formulated in 1965 and still divinely vanillic today. Tom Ford Grey Vetiver is hardly different from Guerlain's Vetiver; in fact, its maker, the aforementioned Harry Fremont, told me Guerlain's was his starting point.

Tom Ford Beau du Jour is incredibly close to Zino Davidoff of 1986 – which is also still available, though in a form slightly less piquant than its first formulation; the creator of Tom Ford Beau du Jour, Antoine Maisondieu, openly told me Zino was his inspiration (I here note, perfunctorily, that Maisondieu is Albert Camus' grandson).

Ultimately, winning a brief, making it into the good graces of a tastemaker, is not necessarily a victory for art – in fact, by the time a perfumer finishes all the requested mods, he or she may find the product far removed from that first creative submission. But there are financial considerations.

Perfumers are paid a base rate – this can be six figures-plus for the industry's biggest names, including stock options – but the real gains come from bonuses.

At Givaudan, your bonus is based in part on how much business – that is, the sale of raw materials based on your formulas – you've brought the firm in aggregate in the prior three years. This sum is then multiplied by a coefficient based on how closely you've matched the targets the company has set for you (one such target may be how many captive – that is, IP-protected – ingredients you've used) and how well your division has performed relative to others (such as the group responsible for food flavors).

One former IFF perfumer told me of another wrinkle in the compensation arrangement. Once a company's perfumers were briefed there on a new development, a fragrance to be launched by Inter Parfums, say, they were privy not just to the potential scent's description but the project's financial forecast – i.e. how much oil (raw material) IFF could sell if it won.

Say, the expectation was $40,000 worth of oil. Well, as the perfumers at IFF all have financial targets to hit, and a $40,000 intake was actually rather small relative to what the big projects brought in, perfumers sometimes chose not to compete to win such a brief. Which sounds mercenary but really is more a matter of practicality: if you'd work equally hard developing one of two fragrances, why concentrate on the one that counts less toward your stipulated oil goal?

It's for this reason that, Olivier Gillotin says, Givaudan asked him not to compete on Tom Ford briefs despite the tremendous success – and heavenly smell – of his Tobacco Vanille, a 2007 release that became the reference vanilla of the century – the accord by which others of the same ilk have all since been measured.[11]

Despite its quality and popularity, this Tom Ford scent was launched in what's known as the "prestige" segment of the market, whose biggest sellers will never yield an oil sale as large as a mass market hit. Gillotin didn't wind up doing another Tom Ford for six years.

Saffron-hued scarf-wearing Olivier Gillotin in his office at Givaudan in New York, a hunk of honey-scented sage wood and a glass canister of vetiver on his desk in the foreground.

If a perfumer doesn't like such corporate diktat, he may jump elsewhere (Gillotin was formerly at IFF), and the best ones, in fact, are urged to do so – recruited by rival concerns. Christophe Raynaud, known for Paco Rabanne 1 Million among other hits, a suave, grey-haired wonderboy, a sort of Gallic Anderson Cooper in appearance, was lured by Firmenich from Givaudan only to have Givaudan entice him to return with a superior package a decade later.

Each fragrance company does believe to some degree that its culture is unique but often for the wrong reasons. Firmenich makes a big deal out of being a private company whose founding family remains involved (Patrick Firmenich is chairman of the board). But I'd argue the great differentiator has always been the array of raw ingredients available to Firmenich perfumers, its chemists having perennially synthesized and isolated the most addictive, enrapturing jasmine components and musks.

Givaudan boasts of its past human relations, when the firm known as Roure was led by a beloved and brilliant perfumer-whisperer who knew how to extract the very best from his charges. But more recently, the firm has been seen by some as unfeeling toward its creators, especially those few masters who, no longer able to rake in the money, were pushed either out the door or into teaching positions at the company's school.

I watched a perfumer at Givaudan whom I love – a perfumer whose natural artistic tendencies extend even to her contemplative emails, which are composed in rhythmic stanzas that proceed like smooth stones along a winding path – a candid sequence of uncertain thoughts – consider for months whether to leave Givaudan for IFF, which was wooing her. The process included chats with IFF's perfumers, a pimping out of IFF's kindest creators by its execs in order to win her over.

I told her about the unique nature of my interviews with IFF perfumers, which were scheduled meticulously by its vice president for "Creation & Design, Branding and Marketing" – Judith Gross – whom I came to adore and respect immensely (and whose rainbow-dyed hair was unique in the industry) but whose initial rigidity – premeditation, say – worried me – she had me email for her review my questions for her company's perfumers the night before each talk (all of which I then conducted via Zoom from my childhood bedroom in my parents' house just outside New York City #PandemicPerfumeChats).

Judith sometimes would request I omit certain queries – or she would suggest I swap out one question for another of her own devisal. If I disagreed with this, I'd argue my case, and she would relent mostly.

All of this was unique to my interactions at IFF — the almost-clinically cold-but information-rich manner in which these perfumers were protected and presented.

So I told my friend, as she pondered whether to leave Givaudan for IFF, about my own experience:

It's good to be empowered by talented people.

But artistry is something that efficiency and industriousness cannot alone produce. In fact, artistry is often found in relaxed places – places that allow for dreaming.

In May 2021, she decided to stay at Givaudan.

Then, the rejection: She absolutely dreaded having to phone up IFF and say no – it felt like listening to a friend vent about having to end a fling. Her email to me immediately once that concluded, composed in small poetic stabs, as her work always is:

The decision I made

Right or wrong

Is my decision

So I have to make it right.

Im just so tired

It's incredible how things like these

Actually drain me of all my energy

I was cold and trembling as I got off the phone

Only months later, she informed me she'd received yet another offer – though she didn't disclose any details except that it intrigued her even more than the last.

Perfumers: pro athletes. Mbappes of odorant mixture but also Griezmanns – offered big money to flip sides but sentimental enough to know when they should not have left at all.

* * *

Dior, Guerlain and Louis Vuitton, all owned by luxury behemoth LVMH, ostensibly operate differently than the above brands – than Tom Ford and Ralph Lauren and Yves Saint Laurent– maintaining in-house perfumers instead of licensing out their names. Cartier, Chanel and Hermes also employ their own noses.

But these perfumers were all hired away from a Givaudan or Firmenich or IFF, to begin with.

The current Chanel perfumer cut his teeth at IFF. Dior's nose worked at smaller firm Mane. Hermes' nose has worked for both Firmenich *and* Givaudan. These luxury houses therefore couldn't produce scent without the scent companies having first hired and honed the talent.

So for better or worse, all processes attendant to creation dissected above – core lists, briefings, oil targets – underpin the work done at these *maisons* with pretensions of aloofness from the industry.

Well, except for Creed and Guerlain – the latter of which dates its founding to 1828 and employed as chief perfumer a male member of the family for more than 150 years – it was not an appointment based on prior achievement but a birthright, the patrimony.

Pierre-François Pascal Guerlain was the first master perfumer and he was followed by Aimé, Jacques and Jean-Paul (all Guerlains), the last of whom held the position into the 1990s, until LVMH took full control of the firm.[12]

That doesn't mean the Guerlains didn't rely on outsider assistance – the 1975 mossy-rose fragrance Parure was handled, in part, by famous IFF hand Ernest Shiftan, who'd co-created Brut a decade earlier. Jean-Paul Guerlain was known for using a different outsider on nearly every project – it was an open secret in the industry – the collaborations indiscreet and spread across several perfumery companies.

Some in-house heroes went unmentioned – such as Anne-Marie

Saget, an airplane pilot, perfumer and Asian toiletries market analyst, who co-authored Guerlain's woody-spicy Derby for gents in 1985 and the sandalwood-heavy Samsara for women in 1989 (whose sandalwood was ordered from Firmenich, another instance of the oil houses clawing their way in just a bit). She left Guerlain on the morning of the latter's release, revulsed by the company's slow and painful reorganization by business school know-it-alls and Louis Vuitton, which had already purchased 14 percent of the company in 1987.[13]

* * *

Creed, by its own account, has always operated in the same manner Guerlain did until the latter's full overtaking by LVMH in 1994. Except Creed had never been purchased – at least, not until I began writing this book, but more on that later – and had entered the business even earlier. And never collaborated with a single outside soul.

Creed says its first perfume was released in the 18th century – Royal English Leather of 1781, authored by one James Henry Creed. All fragrances since have similarly been composed by his male descendants, including Olivier Creed since the beginning of the 1970s and Olivier's son Erwin since the turn of the Millennium.

Creed is happy to provide reporters with the names of figures it has fragranced in this incredible span of time. A 1993 Les Echoes article lists as clients: Queen Victoria, Napoleon III, Empress Eugenie, Christine of Spain, Jean Rochefort, Philippe Noiret and Robert Redford.[14] A Town & Country magazine article says Sigmund Freud ordered a custom Creed scent in 1901.[15]

Creed's own Web site supplements this roster with further boldfaced names – primarily from the Golden Age of Hollywood:

Angelique Encens was created for Marlene Dietrich in 1933 and "remained her favourite fragrance for the rest of her life." Cuir de

Russie was created for Errol Flynn in 1938, Fleur de The Rose Bulgare for Ava Gardner in 1948. Jasmal for Natalie Wood in 1959. Selection Verte was made for Cary Grant in 1955, as was Green Irish Tweed 30 years later, or just before Grant died.

It's hard to know which feat here is more impressive – the consistent development of scents so alluring that the world's most famous figures of each generation desired them or that not once during this period was the family under the sort of pressure Guerlain felt so keenly in the '90s to have outsiders work on their scents to save the business.

Examine 1995 – a year Guerlain was in much turmoil, as LVMH forced Jean-Paul Guerlain now to compete with outside perfumers – from Firmenich and Givaudan – to win briefs, a development an uninformed New York Times Magazine article of that year nevertheless managed to reflect by accident, calling Jean-Paul the "nose" of the "venerable house" under the headline "Still Going" in a magazine section titled – wait for it – "Appearances."[16]

But 1995 at Creed saw the release of Silver Mountain Water, a sparkling tea and black currant fragrance ostensibly inspired by Olivier's championship alpine skiing – the firm never disclosed which championships its literature referred to – and crafted by him alone, *sans* outside consultation or competition.

Unlike any new Guerlain release from that year – and there was just one, a lighter variation of the Samsara scent released in 1989 – Silver Mountain Water is still on sale, though that term may not be the best choice of words in this context, given the pricing of the product. Silver Mountain Water retails for $415 per 3.3 oz. bottle at perfume web site luckyscent.com, for $660.00 for an 8.4 oz. decanter at Saks and for $1,005.00 for a 17 oz. dram at Bloomingdale's.

Just how does Creed, both the man and the firm, operating differently than everyone else in the industry, devise scents of such originality and timeliness they can charge these prices and find consumers eager to pay them?

Or put another way, if their methods work so well, why haven't oil houses and licensee firms attempted to adopt them?

And how does a company manage both to predate and survive all others in its field without ever for a moment having fallen out of fashion, even among Tinseltown elite and royal families?

How *does* perfumery work?

Olivier Creed sniffs a fragrance blotter ("mouillette," en français) at his brand's counter at Barneys, in New York, 1999. (Courtesy Chang W. Lee/The New York Times/Redux)

Chapter 3: The Inheritance of Olivier Creed

I *'m like a psychoanalyst," muses the French-born Creed, 56, who started working for his father in the family business when he was 19...* "The Sweet Smell of Excess," Forbes, Oct. 10, 1999

You know on TV, when a child is about to be snatched by a stranger at a pool or park or playground, the camera focuses on the kid but too intently, and it's just this overly-engaged visual that tips us off: Someone's gonna abduct this kid – because no parent, even a most watchful one – would pay that sort of breathy, unblinking attention?

Who hasn't, at one point, said, *What did I just miss?*

Is this the secret to the incredibly unquestioned revisionism of Olivier Creed? That he dared onlookers to blame themselves – admit the limits of their observation – with such rollicking, rococo recounting?

I could've sworn he was just a tailor, one might say, *but nobody would falsify 300 years of history simply for the sake of...of what, even? More money than a rich inheritor already has? Prestige? A false feeling of accomplishment?*

And one would be reasonable to ask, as well: *How can a person whose life is predicated on such a deception derive from it anything but self-doubt?*

Consider this: What if Creed, having come to believe his own contrivance, is the liar who passes the polygraph?

* * *

A man by the name of James Henry Creed, having first found employ cleaning the horse stables of Leicestershire, England, later launched a clothing business in 1760, at least according to a book written 200 hundred years later (not that I've reason to disbelieve this version of the family lineage, though it sounds altogether too neat in the aforementioned book, but then, most history books do).

Apparently, each successive generation of Creeds stuck to their namesake apparel business, which the family moved from London to Paris in 1854.

Olivier Creed was born nearly 100 years later, in 1943, in Nice – an heir to this tailoring tradition but more than that, a product of a family schism, the split between his father and uncle in the previous generation.

His uncle, Charles, caroused drunkenly, suffered from gout by the time of his honeymoon and spent his World War II service time much like Gould and Sutherland in "MASH" or James Garner in "The Americanization of Emily," always in search of available bottles (or barrels) of booze (in emptied cities retaken by the Allies).

None of this pleased his stodgy father, who refused to hand over his Paris shop to this wastrel son. Lucky for Pops, he had another option, an heir more trustworthy and reliable – James Henry (yes, he shared the name of the legendary family progenitor, to boot). It was decided that the prodigal son Charles would focus on womenswear in a London boutique in Knightsbridge while James Henry would pursue men's furnishings in Paris at the historic family shop at 7 Rue Royale (next to Maxim's, once considered the most famous restaurant in the world).

And so Charles left Paris – one might say, he was banished from it – cut off from the family fortune to the degree that he sometimes relied on his wife's family for funding (or perhaps he was still pulling in a nice bit of Creed family remittances but was too profligate to rely on those – and his own couture proceeds – alone; the bottom line is that he leaned on his in-laws for cash).

Yet in London, Charles Creed did become part of a famous generation of prim women's clothiers, sometimes called the "Big 10," on whose lives director Paul Thomas Anderson based the character Reynolds Woodcock in the 2017 film "Phantom Thread."

In fact, there was always something showbiz – dazzling – about Charles Creed's life – from his Hollywood meetings with gossip columnist Hedda Hopper to the Victoria and Albert Museum's accepting and staging his work for posterity. Even England's National Portrait Gallery holds two photographs of Charles Creed.

And Charles' reputation for fine work and finer living was only bolstered by his marriage to the fashion editor of British Vogue and his more temporary carnal attachments to a series of models (when Charles died of a heart attack in 1966, his wife was elsewhere – in Rome, working for shoe designer Salvatore Ferragamo).

CHARLES CREED

DJ 707

Destined to be one of the most attractive ensembles of the season—because it combines elegance with neatness and because it is so versatile from Afternoons into Evenings. Created with the distinctive flair of Charles Creed in a new wool 'basket weave' tweed with a contrasting bolero top in velvet—also on the jacket cuffs, collar and buttons. Duck Egg Blue or Winter White with Brown Velvet.

Sizes 12-18. About 12½ gns.

For the name of your nearest stockist, please write to
Charles Creed (London) Ltd.,
33 Maddox Street, London. W.1.

An ad for Charles Creed's couture—the subject's pose — those pursed lips — indicative of Charles' rather sensual manner. (Courtesty of AgeFotoStock/Mary Evans Picture Library)

By contrast, there's nothing in the public record I could find to suggest the other brother – James Henry Creed – who was handed the Paris shop, lived a life of great fascination or celebrity or excess. He was not a boldfaced name. In fact, according to his brother's memoir, James Henry was something of a scold.

At Charles' wedding, at the altar, James Henry said to his brother, *the bloody groom*, in French, "I can't understand why you want to marry this woman at all!"

To which Patricia Cunningham, bride and fluent French speaker, replied: "Perhaps, there is a streak of insanity in your family?"

Meanwhile, as the brothers jousted with each other from opposite sides of the Channel, they were also cultivating their own backup, as it were. For Charles, the eternally roguish man-child, this meant collecting lead and porcelain Napoleonic toy soldiers – a collection that gathered notice.

For James Henry, this meant producing a male heir to take over the Paris business, known formally as H. Creed. This he did – but with an unforeseen result: The son he raised and trained for the task, Olivier, didn't care much for tailoring. He had sufficient capacity but no enthusiasm.

Actually, Olivier's taste for the high life mirrored his uncle's disposition much more than his father's (so far as the research about his father permits me to conclude). And so, Olivier Creed, handsome but dutiful young man, perhaps faced the world with a split psyche: He wanted to party like his uncle yet keep promises made to his father.

Playboy designer Charles Creed, Olivier's uncle, posing with a model in the March 1953 issue of British Vogue. (photograph by Norman Parkinson; courtesy of Iconic Images)

Whether this divide caused Olivier to begin lying – or he was a fabulist from birth – I cannot say – although some evidence would suggest he was a born tale-teller, such as his interview with Le Figaro in 2007 in which he admitted he was indeed also a clothier once (a rare admission) but decided to list, of all the Creed clients in the world, two men of such great notoriety and so little else in common – the Shah of Iran and the mobster Lucky Luciano[17] — one senses already an unlikeliness in the recollection, the ease of a tongue indifferent to the truth, unbound by its demands.

That impression is furthered by Creed's 2008 mention of his education in the finer arts, which, even if true, has the feel of a reverse-dog-ate-my-homework plea or the Jon Lovitz SNL act – *yeah, that's the ticket*:

"I learned painting in school, and I painted more than 100 canvasses before becoming master perfumer...Georges Braque was a neighbor of ours, and I was fortunate to paint with him upon occasion."[18]

(Oh, and the journalist to whom Creed was talking about Braque was told Creed hadn't given an interview to anyone in 15 years, despite Olivier's having just namedropped the Shah and the mafioso the year before – and having never ceased to speak practically ever.)

But even if these stories point to something amiss in the mind of Olivier, a tendency *confabulatoire* more innate than acquired, one can nevertheless see perfumery as a compromise between the staid business bequeathed him by his father and the fast life limned so enticingly by his uncle in the gossip pages.

In fact, even the New York Times, that grave broadsheet, noted on its Society page ever so smugly – too clever by half: "Charles Creed" – Olivier's uncle — "has not lost his flair for tailor-mades – or, for that matter, for tailored maids."[19]

Fragrance was a fabric-adjacent product – an item not unknown in men's haberdasheries – but one evocative of a garment's removal – of a carnality that begins where clothing ends. No one in the family had done it before (so far as the record indicates) and yet it could be sold among the accessories as if it always had.

What better middle ground for a young man seeking sexiness from a musty, fusty tweed patrimony?

Or...perhaps it wasn't such a hormonal affair, someone in the family *had* managed the bottling of a lame, utterly unexceptional cologne at some prior point, which had long sat accumulating dust in a dark recess of the 7 Rue Royale shop – lord knows who devised it, but the well-to-do Creeds had friends in fancy places – and this product being so utterly devoid of worth, survived by no attestations to its smell and style (unlike every product of this era from Guerlain, Chanel, Caron... etc), its very existence remaining highly in doubt, Olivier's enterprise was less impulsive than inspired – a kind of cerebral challenge: How can I make relevant the least interesting item within my ken?

Or perhaps, as Creed's former US distributor, Laurice Rahme, told me, Olivier Creed's perfume gambit was the product of greed or power-hunger – the rich wanting to be richer, the rich wanting to be rulers. Maybe it was math: Olivier lusted after the exceptional margins on perfume.

"I wonder who could talk to you about this, the motivation," Laurice added. "I tell you who could, but I don't know if she would. It's his ex-wife. The ex-wife because now he's with another woman. The mother of Erwin. The first wife, Fabienne. She was in charge of the store in Paris...She would call me and say, 'Take care of my son. His father is nasty.'"

But that's skipping ahead some. Because when Olivier Creed launched his life in perfumery he was just 20 years old. The year was 1963, and he'd set out from Paris for Lille, to a small shop called Soleil d'Or that had been open a decade.

Creed himself has acknowledged this trip on a couple of occasions – perhaps out of sheer hubris, his fear of being found out entirely dissipated (not unlike his character, I'd say, if I really thought Creed was evil instead of entitled, imperious and given to lying so compulsively it's beyond a matter of morals, even if it is utterly amoral).

A current employee of the Soleil d'Or confirmed the visit and the year for me, as well – although that itself gave me pause.

Soleil d'Or still retails Creed bottles, every one of which is marked prominently with the ostensible founding year of 1760, or three decades prior to the French Revolution, even though the shopkeeper, Sandy Picavet, acknowledges Olivier didn't arrive with bottles until at least 1963, or the year the Beatles recorded their first LP in a single, all-day session at Abbey Road.

Either the Creed family maintained a secret perfume operation of the highest standard for 200 years (which is its occasional claim, incidentally – that its fragrances were vended only to royals, sub rosa) or Soleil d'Or is doing what every other shop has done in relation to Creed, only with precise knowledge of the incongruities – they're promulgating a self-serving myth.

I don't fault them; I pity them the condition of their trade. And Sandy Picavet, the one who works there and assisted me, was nothing but kind.

"We were indeed the first to sell Creed perfumes and their custom-made men's suits," Sandy emailed me. "At the time, no one knew Creed, Olivier Creed himself came to present his brand, as did many perfume and cosmetic brands which took their *first steps* in our perfumery."

The italics are mine.

But why did Olivier Creed choose the Soleil d'Or?

His own bizarre admission in 2013, which nobody besides me seems to have picked up on, hardly flatters the shop:

"When I was starting out — this would be back in the 1960s – people were not always encouraging. Some retailers would say, well, we already have Chanel and Dior (fragrances), why should we bother with you? I remember going to Lille. Okay, so we are talking about a northern [industrial] French city with a population of 300,000."[20]

Olivier Creed, to Le Figaro in 2013: "When I entered with my creations exclusively in a *provincial* perfume store like Le Soleil d'Or, in Lille, in 1963, it was a real challenge against the big brands."[21]

Translation: *Perfumery was a brand new business for us, so I chose to soft-launch it in the sticks.* One mystery solved. But he calls these perfumes "my creations." How could that even be?

The company claims that its latest scents in 1963 – and this is taking Creed's patently falsified records at face value – had been concocted by Olivier's father in 1956 and 1953 – or when Olivier was 13 and 10 years old. So even by their own family accounting, one has to wonder: what in the hell juice did Olivier actually convey up there, under the label "my creations"?

And then there's the small claim of his success. "It was a real challenge to the big brands," we've heard him tell Le Figaro. "Three years later, in Lille, we were doing as much business as Guerlain," he told The Independent.[22]

It could be true. But Creed let slip to a French cosmetics magazine that the company was selling just 1,200 bottles per year in 1970 – or seven years after his first trip to Lille and the introduction of his product to the market.[23]

But there's another version of this story – this one written by the daughter of the Soleil d'Or founders – a couple that ran a café for 20 years before tiring of that business and adopting an utterly unalike, if no less aromatic, one in 1953. The book wasn't hard to obtain: The Soleil d'Or sent me a beautiful copy printed in 2006, *gratis*.

Page 41: "But what interests Olivier [as opposed to tailoring] are the perfumes. The first, those he presents to us, he has them made according to his own inspiration: Tabarome, Cypres-Musc, Bayrhum Vetiver."

"Has them made" – an indication from the very first vendor of Creed fragrances – perhaps by slip of the tongue/typewriter – that Olivier commissions rather than creates them.

And then, there's the impossible chronology. Olivier Creed and his company claim Tabarome (now called Tabarome Prive) was made in 1875 and later worn by Winston Churchill. Cypres-Musc and Bayrhum Vetiver are both dated to 1948, the year Olivier turned 5.

How, in the words of the perfume store's own annals, could these products have been made according to Olivier's "own inspiration" if they were truly as old as Creed claims? The Soleil d'Or further makes the case quite accidentally for Creed's backdating, for a distortion of time no less imaginative than H.G. Wells'. Again, page 41, on these first three Olivier-presented scents:

"They anticipate everything that will characterize his future creations: originality, classicism, simplicity, a mark of real good taste."

If true, and the fragrances bear Olivier's own imprint, their formulation can't possibly have predated his adulthood or birth. But okay, let's ignore their origin and ask instead, if they were distinguished by "originality, classicism, simplicity," how well they sold in this Lille shop.

"It was more difficult to offer than the perfumes that carried a known name."

Well that line neither accords with the centuries of renown Creed (man and company) claim nor Olivier's assessment that his stuff swiftly sold as many bottles as Guerlain.

But page 53 in this history arguably offers a keener insight into the business and brains of Olivier Creed during this mid-century period – this early adulthood spell when his future was perhaps still undecided, when his character remained unsettled (unless he was congenitally unethical).

Page 53 marks Creed's entrance into the Lille establishment – into an expansion of Le Soleil d'Or undertaken in 1975 – to that bell-bottom annum, which is actually a launch year some historians find plausible (the oldest Creed in the collection of the Osmothèque, a facility that preserves historical fragrances in Versailles, dates to 1975). Moreover, it underlines that Creed's activity in the wing was sartorial instead of olfactive to start, to that point that Olivier's tailoring venture was replaced instead by a display of men's fragrances:

"Pierre (the uncle of the author and so a member of the family that ran the shop) announces to us that he wants to market 'Creed' tailor-made couture for men. But after several months, it is clear that it does not work. Pierre is very disappointed, but we are installing the men's eau de toilette department there. Now with hindsight, it was a good decision since that's what kept us going."

And there it is: Having no desire to be a men's haberdasher, Creed nevertheless, at least once, tried his hand at it beyond the safer confines of his family shop and failed – failed in a parochial area he considered beneath him. Moreover, he'd brought along fragrance of sketchy provenance, likely assembled by others (but certainly not before his birth) or just maybe concocted independently, and he had not matched Guerlain in sales – or Dior or Chanel – all perfumeries to which he'd made comparison.

Which means if Creed wanted to continue in the fragrance sphere – and I don't doubt his enthusiasm back then for scent, even if its origin was a hunger for power – he now needed a new plan: Perhaps a more extensive brand mythology, sure, but fragrances of exceptional quality to back up such a tale.

Where could he obtain such singular scent? Or put more precisely, from whom?

Chapter 4: The Education of Pierre Bourdon

"There are many people who believe that Pierre Bourdon might be the greatest perfumer of all time."
— Dale Dewey, CEO of the first online perfume retailer

When the Great War ended in 1919, Rene Bourdon, a 7 year-old boy born in Crennes, Normandy, welcomed back from the front a father who'd become alcoholic, his superiors having forced him to drink for courage before they stormed out of the trenches.

Unable to continue working in his former profession as a plasterer, the father was soon committed to a hospice. That left the task of earning money to Rene's mother, who took odd jobs as a housecleaner and seamstress.

One day, searching for his mother about the house, Rene finally found her in the attic – by herself hanged, a dangling, lifeless corpse. Rene was not yet 12.

A priest found an adoptive family for Rene in the Auvergne region of central France – a family that had lost its own son to the war. Rene learned stenography and typing before his enlistment in the French forces in World War II, and it was his captain who, impressed with the lad's wit, according to family lore, found him employment in peacetime at a Féret Frères, a toiletries and perfumery concern with the sole distribution rights to such brands as Nivea, Colgate, and Bayer.

Rene took business management courses in the evening and thus made himself a desirable hire for Serge Heftler-Louiche, a childhood friend of Christian Dior who in 1947 was assembling for the fashion designer a proper perfume operation – known as Parfums Christian Dior.

Rene Bourdon was made deputy director general and, later, general manager responsible for the development of new products.

This latter task demanded Rene's judgment on the works of master perfumers, a major charge for a young man and one paralleled by a new personal duty: A year after the war ended, he'd had a son with a gymnastics teacher he had met in Toulouse. They called the boy Pierre, and the family settled in the 17th arrondissement of Paris, in an apartment overlooking the Square des Batignolles.

Rene Bourdon was now overseer of a premier French cultural institution – or at least, a firm that so viewed itself – and a small family. And if he confused the two accounts, so that members of the latter were often held to the severe standards he helped set in the former, well, that was to both the great fortune and detriment of his little boy, who'd come to understand young just what was considered an artistic contribution worthy of Dior's imprimatur – and all the brilliant work that, for any number of reasons never shared, either with the boy regarding his homework or perfumer-aspirants their trials, was not.

Whether one can forgive Rene this mistake is really beside the point – it's for the son to choose to pardon his pops, always – but one can certainly understand it. Rene Bourdon had no reference point for how to be a parent because he had none himself. His father returned from World War I an alcoholic with PTSD and no capacity to care for himself, let alone his family. Then his mother committed suicide. If his greatest sin was treating Pierre not like a son but an insufficiently capable artist – to the degree, in fact, that he told his son merely twice that he loved him – when the son turned 50 and as the father literally lay dying –because love doesn't enter into the equation when you're evaluating art for commercial release – he was guilty not of misrule but of misunderstanding. Of choosing the wrong paradigm for parenting, because there was no prior Bourdon precedent for how it's done.

Which isn't to minimize the yearning the boy must have felt for affection of a filial nature. To go through a lifetime without it done right – it must have been tremendously upsetting, though Pierre even now doesn't expound greatly on that topic. Pierre's quiet itself speaks volumes, however, and always has.

He was a sensitive, obedient and lonely boy, who took pleasure in the usual pursuits of the bright introvert – he read great books and listened to classical music – plus an endeavor uniquely available to a child in his flat: Sniffing the trials of perfumers in advance of new releases – the greatest experience of which, by his own account, involved the assays of master Edmond Roudnitska for Dior's seminal men's fragrance Eau Sauvage (recalled now for its incorporation of the jasmine isolate hedione, which in 2015 scientists discovered induces arousal in women).[24]

But Pierre was not entirely marked by his homelife, such that his father's assessments held complete sway over the boy. Pierre was still intelligent and inquisitive, if quiet, and attended a sufficiently rigorous all-boys high school that he came across plenty lessons to pique that natural curiosity.

His most profound influence was French and Latin teacher Andre Giachetti, who was a prominent scholar of Medieval texts. In fact, the University of Rouen published his translation of an anonymous Arthurian proto-novel from the 15th century called "Ysaïe le Triste" – Isaiah the Sad – about two knights errant and their little valet Tronq;

spoiler alert: Tronq turns out to have been a supernatural being the entire time.

Giachetti excited Bourdon with his erudition and enthusiasm. This "Dead Poets Society"-type played Beethoven to bring to life the beginning of Stendhal's "The Charterhouse of Parma." He had the class stage Jean Racine's play "Andromaque." And Pierre recalls reading in this era Camus, Sartre, Mauriac, Henry de Montherlant, André Gide, Hervé Bazin, Romain Rolland, André Malraux, Saint-John Perse, F. Scott Fitzgerald, Faulkner, Steinbeck, Dylan Thomas.

And when Pierre finished first in the class, Giachetti gifted him a copy of "Le Grand Meaulnes," the only novel written by Henri Alain-Fournier before the author was killed in the first month of World War I – a valedictory gift rife with symbolism. Pierre's grandfather and grandmother both lost their lives to that war (indirectly but still), and his father's mishandling of childrearing was the consequence. Now, Pierre's idol was handing him a novel by a dead soldier – one that happens to be about the end of adolescence, the golden period of innocent play and trysts before we lose our lighter selves to an inescapably weighty world.

Could the gift had been more fitting – more apropos of the events that had brought Pierre to that moment in time? Hardly, and yet, Pierre was left wondering what such connections ultimately meant. His tragic backstory, its ripples through time, his artistic disposition – what did it all amount to now that Pierre had to make his own life decisions?

And so he initially went with the easy choice – the default: He'd not move on at all – he'd stay where he already knew he could thrive – he'd study to become a French literature teacher and return, become a Giachetti for future generations of curious, quiet, brilliant boys.

But Rene Bourdon argued a teacher's salary was insufficient, and Pierre conceded, matriculating for university at The Paris Institute of

Political Studies, more commonly called Sciences Po and one of the country's most prestigious schools, its Ivy League-level offering.

This resolved for now Pierre's financial future – at least in his father's mind – any number of companies would hire a graduate of such an institution. But there was an aspect of Pierre's development that seemed anything but settled to him, and this the son mulled without needing any external prodding.

Getting some.

He'd read the books about young love (aren't they all?), but his had been a single-sex school, and even if it hadn't, he was still sufficiently reserved a character as to put in doubt whether he'd have made it with a female pupil during those formative years.

Now he was 18 – of age – and it was high time he discovered directly just what sex was all about.

Fortunately, a love of language and art that might've been held against him just a few years earlier was now considered an asset by the opposite sex – especially young women of a similar nature who'd always wanted to say as much but had lacked the confidence to make an overture themselves.

This Pierre found out plainly when a girl he'd met on a language study trip to Germany a couple years earlier, who lived in his Paris neighborhood and was herself still a virgin, insinuated her way into his life, so that they began meeting surreptitiously, in order not to have explain to their parents just what they were doing (at a stage when they were still figuring out how it's even done).

If Pierre had taken more cues from his reading, he'd probably have imagined a way to stage these secret liaisons in some unsuspectingly sexy spot, one whose grunge would make him seem all the more roguish – lend him a certain Byronic flair.

As it happened, fumbling and in heat, they had sex for the first time on the filthy floor of a maid's room, the setting neither enhancing his aura nor the act itself. This set the pattern for their subsequent encounters, all of which occurred amidst the wrong kind of dirt. The wrong kind of dirt: a motel room can feel a rousingly outre arrangement or one simply seedy. So.

And repetition did the dynamic no favors – the ebbing of first enthusiasms allowing a more clear-eyed view of wanting circumstance. So she terminated their fling, which didn't bother Pierre, at least not in his recollection. He was joyous for having gotten off the mark.

At Sciences Po, Pierre majored in economics and finance but fell ill with a condition then known in France as "Réticulose X," a systemic hyperactivity of the immune system, not far removed from cancer. Unenrolled from classes for a year, Pierre began reading Proust's "À la recherche du temps perdu," which, utterly changing his values, led him to a Schopenhauerian conception of life as an inherently worthless thing, kept going by wants and needs of our own invention, transcended only by art, by a contemplation of things that makes us one with them.

This reading accounted partly for Pierre's choice of profession; his father's design accounted for the rest.

Pierre "posing as a dandy," in the words of his present wife, while at uni.

One day, Rene invited Pierre to accompany him on a weekend business trip to the house of genius perfumer Edmond Roudnitska in Cabris, in the Maritime Alps, in the south of France.

Roudnitska, his work part science and part artistry, was the rare fellow who truly impressed Rene. Is it any wonder that he impressed the son, too?

Pierre found Roudnitska to be a man of strong personality and difficult character – that is, a man undoubtedly endowed with the temperament of an artist. The son was additionally seduced by Roudnitska's lifestyle: he lived in a large modern house filled with works of art and abutted by a lovely garden, all of it overlooking the bay of Cannes. The house offered the most magnificent panoramic view of the Riviera Pierre had ever beheld. Pierre's father told him additionally that Roudnitska worked just two hours a day and spent the rest of his schedule writing and playing sports.

On the trip back home, Pierre told his father he would become a perfumer, which news delighted the older man, even if it didn't entirely surprise him (although to this day, Pierre wonders just how set his father was on this outcome; he never found out for sure whether the whole trip was orchestrated with just this one endpoint as its goal; he never really quizzed Rene on the degree of his calculations; now, it's too late).

Once Pierre Bourdon told his father of his perfumer-aspiration, Rene spoke to the raw materials houses whose business depended on Dior's patronage (these are sometimes called "oil houses," as a perfume's ingredients are an oil until cut with a percentage of alcohol). He returned to Pierre with two choices: he could attend the perfumery school at Givaudan, one of the two major flavor and fragrance firms based in Switzerland, or that of Roure in Grasse, France, a hamlet on the Riviera thick with jasmine and rose. He chose the latter for its superior climate and accommodations.

The Roure curriculum had students learn to distinguish raw materials in a particular order – first those whose aromas were quite obviously dissimilar and then later those with more subtle differences. This method of studying had been devised by Jean Carles, the Roure perfumer who also invented the fragrance pyramid – the now-common device of breaking down a perfume into top, mid and base notes, based on their relative rates of dissipation.

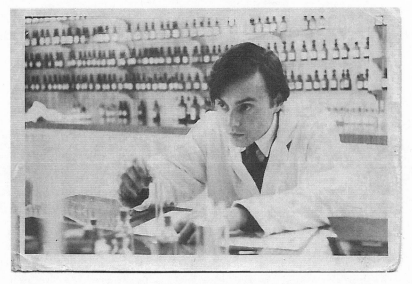

Pierre at the Roure school in the 1970s.

Bourdon visited Dior perfumer Edmond Roudnitska twice a week during his five year-stay in Grasse. By his own account, Bourdon was the only disciple Roudnitska ever took on, though Jean-Claude Ellena, later the in-house perfumer for Hermes, was a familial relation of the master and emulated his style.

"We have in common our adoption of his precepts of composition," Bourdon says of him and Ellena and Roudnitska. "We are his heirs."

Heirs: The Roure school had always been small, clubby and dominated by men, and so Bourdon only had three female classmates, one of whom, a certain Francoise Cresp, came from a local family with roots in the perfume industry (her brother would invent a whole new genre of perfumery – the food-evoking "gourmands" decades later).

As Bourdon had begun studying perfumery far later than his peers – having attended first a university – and Francoise had a native's knowledge of the trade – he had to work double-time to keep up, while she could afford to fall into a more languorous rhythm – to live as she learned, to indulge her senses even as she honed one in particular.

This contrast inevitably led to enmity between boy and girl – she poked fun at his serious manner, as though it were a rebuke of her more relaxed course. He found this more obnoxious than funny and didn't hesitate to let her know.

After three months of discord – love and hate being alike impassioned – they found themselves in bed together.

Heirs: Bourdon — by his account — quite unintentionally impregnated Francoise, which impelled them to marry, at a cathedral in Grasse – a turn of events that benefited Pierre's education in the short term. His new father-in-law, an expert in raw materials, took him Saturday afternoons to a warehouse to teach him how to recognize jasmines of multiple origins, to differentiate between batches of bergamot harvested during the same season, "as well as all the secrets of his profession," in Pierre's words.

"I owe him a precious complement of my training," Pierre says.

All this education, formal and makeshift, was merely prelude to Pierre and Francoise taking posts as actual Roure perfumers – positions handed a select few in the 1970s.

At the time Roure occupied just two offices, one in Paris on the short Rue Jacques Bingen, just yards away from a small park with a monument to Alexandre Dumas, in the 17th Arrondissement, and another just outside the capital, in Argenteuil.

When Pierre Bourdon and Francoise moved north, these headquarters were occupied by highly accomplished fine fragrance figures. Raymond Chaillan had done work on Givenchy III for women in 1970 and authored Balenciaga Ho Hang for men in '71, Yves Saint Laurent Pour Homme that same year, plus Molyneux Quartz and Monsieur Carven at the end of the Seventies.[25]

And though the record books often overlook this, Chaillan had already contributed a great deal to what would become Yves Saint Laurent's Opium (specifically the mandarin orange, carnation and spice accords).

Then there was Jean-Louis Sieuzac, the man who brought an aldehyde accord to the head of Opium and is usually credited with its final formula. Sieuzac had also done a scent for Max Factor and another for Oscar de la Renta.

And Francoise Marin — a woman perfumer like Bourdon's own wife – which is to say, someone quite strong, given the prevailing mores of the day (and even now) – had worked with Chaillan to adapt American perfume formulas for the French market (and vice-versa). Marin would go on to lead the Roure training school from which Pierre and his other half had just graduated.

But the most important new colleague of the married couple was their boss, Jean Amic, whose father, Louis, had run Roure before him. Jean Amic was perceived by some Roure old-hands as an undeserving playboy, a nepotistic hire whose rakish appeal to women would never extend to the firm's clients (that he boasted such sexual appeal even while resembling Buck Henry testifies to Jean Amic's charisma).

Yet nearly everyone empowered in the fragrance world must first overcome such prejudice – a perfumer paranoia of the "other" born in part of self-doubt, in an industry whose brightest minds lose briefing contests nine times out of 10. In fact, Pierre Bourdon himself was first seen by at least one Roure colleague as a legacy hire, handed a role merely because of his father's status at Dior.

But Jean Amic was perfectly suited to the quasi-creative gig of running an oil house – he was both hard-minded and philosophical. Though a Grasse native, had attended MIT for college, graduating in 1956 with a math degree. He'd then told his father – the sixth-generation of their family to run Roure – that he preferred to win a job on merit instead of heredity and went to work for Goodyear, setting up the tire company's French operation.

In 1962 – here's his loverboy side – Amic married a Romanian princess. When he finally joined Roure a few years later, it was to lead its American operation. In the following two decades, Jean took control of the entire company from his father, with spectacular results, such that by the late 1980s, this tiny Grasse raw materials firm was doing $100 million in sales each year. And all the while, the eccentric Amic was reading up on anthropology, the history of civilizations, behavioral science.

A 1986 article in Women's Wear Daily about Amic and his wife, Irene, said Jean "is a serious, straight-shooting man with a moody metaphysical bent," adding, "he is also a loner."

Said Irene in the piece, "Jean is interested in the evolution of the world, a curiosity which, if you're anguished, is quite normal."

Well, if you're anguished...

An anonymous friend on Amic: "He's exactly like he wants to be. If he doesn't want to be nice, he doesn't make the effort."

This Jean Amic – well-credentialed, confident, blunt, meditative, wary of humans yet fascinated by humanity – he was now the boss of Bourdon of and his wife Francoise.

Amic was a "pleasant boss," Raymond Chaillan recalled for me in a recent email. "He appreciated his perfumers, motivated them, took an interest in their work, followed them, sometimes guided them, knew the raw materials well and had an excellent nose. The last boss perfumer! Like his father, an excellent salesman."

Bourdon calls Amic "the best salesman of his time and a peerless evaluator." And though Bourdon had no desire yet to leave Roure – having only just arrived – he nevertheless observed Amic's "commercial practices," which he'd work to replicate on his own when, in not too many years' time, he'd find himself competing with Amic, essentially running his own oil house. But that was all ahead of Bourdon – for now he was watching simply to learn.

"He was the only boss that I admired" Bourdon says, "despite his cynicism, which was not his most pleasant character trait, especially when he regularly provoked his perfumers by telling them: 'You are not artists but specialized workers!'

"Besides, he paid us so badly that half of the perfumers trained at Roure deserted to earn more elsewhere and thus reinforced the competition which ended up triumphing over him."

Of course, as Bourdon formed impressions of his new colleagues, they, too, were sizing him up – and his wife Francoise besides. One perfumer found Bourdon "cold, not frank, scheming," and Francoise a person utterly lacking in confidence, to the point that she'd cry about an inability to fulfill her remit (despite having created several gorgeous scents since, Francois is said to be unduly diffident still; she credits her 1981 Ombre Rose for Jean-Charles Brosseau to Pierre – as does he – even though other perfumers can sense her personal aesthetic – her style of construction – in the formula).

Was Bourdon as cocky as he seemed? Hardly. But bookishness can be confused for hauteur – a loner mentality for aloofness. And it didn't help that his father was the well-known manager of Parfums Dior. In truth, Bourdon respected his colleagues and was rather abashed about the prospect of competing with them to win briefs. He didn't want to tear down his peers to achieve success nor be sacrificed likewise for the enrichment of another.

So Bourdon pulled out of this royal rumble, asking overlord Jean Amic whether he could devote himself to toiletries – the creation of scent for deodorants, shampoos, hairsprays, soaps and shower gels. He further decided to request an exclusive territory one waterway north of the Gallic scrum: England.

And so the once enfeebled-Proustian, whose sexual awakening occurred in a dim dingy worker's warren, made his olfactive mark in the bathrooms of British women – not that they knew for a moment who'd scented their soaps...or the status this man would soon attain.

Pierre's rise in perfumery came about quite by accident, in fact. It was the late 1970s, after Roure's success creating Yves Saint Laurent's Opium for women, and now YSL was looking for a new masculine, a scent with commensurate commercial impact – for the men's wholesale fragrance market was suddenly a $300 million affair. And those department store buyers so crucial to the success of Opium wanted a men's counterpart for their own pecuniary reasons: Perfume counters priced prestige men's scents 90 percent higher than the wholesale costs.[26]

The expense for YSL to develop such a masculine fragrance, then? A mere $5 to $10 million, including everything from formulation to packaging to marketing.[27] The economics weren't just enticing – they were irresistible.

Pierre Bourdon was *not* initially briefed on the YSL male project – which was codenamed "Eros." But then Jean Amic realized Roure was going to lose this brief to a competitor, so he burst into Bourdon's office one morning and said:

"Get me the formula for your imitation of Matchabelli's Cachet and make it masculine."

What this meant: Cachet was a women's perfume launched a decade prior, in June 1970, that sold very well in England – the territory Bourdon controlled at Roure. But it had been created by a perfumer at Firmenich – Roure's rival in the fragrance business.

At some point, then, in order to grasp better how this scent worked its magic, Bourdon had made a study of it – had tried to deconstruct and rebuild it in his own lab – a practice common in the industry then and now. So Bourdon had possession of the Cachet formula, more or less.

What Amic badly wanted was a "twist" – something that would take a decade-old women's bestseller and lend it a contemporary and manly appeal. Bourdon was well aware this was possible – he knew that Aramis, Lauder's male hit of the mid '60s, had actually been based on the feminine Cabochard by Gres of 1959. And that Brut, the iconic midcentury aftershave, owed its structure to Canoe by Dana, the 1930s women's hit authored by the father of the Roure training school, Jean Carles.

But just because Bourdon understood this method of working didn't mean he felt it appropriate here. In fact, he considered it an absurd notion, born of Amic's panic – but one didn't argue with the boss unless one planned on leaving Roure – which Bourdon would indeed do in mere months – though he had no idea about that yet.

For now, he worked on grafting elements of a popular men's hit onto the Cachet core – Paco Rabanne Pour Homme of 1973 (which, as mentioned earlier, is the fragrance my father wore in his bachelor days and which cost $15 in the late 1970s – at the low end of the prestige category).[28] And lest one think all of this was thievery, it should be noted that Bourdon took steps even to make his Cachet more like the 1947 perfume Miss Dior – remember now that his father still worked at Dior and never gave the boy the validation he craved. A regression to Dior was a choice not entirely stylistic: Its presence in the Father was almost an imploring: Please look, Pops — I can do this as well!

But Pierre was feeling himself very much a man in these days for reasons soon to be elaborated, despite those moments of boyish neediness. And so he added some real dude odor to the formula – a product called Animalis from the raw material supplier Synarome that contained para-cresyl phenyl acetate, a compound chemists say smells of animals and urine and feces.[29]

The overall product – Animalis in its entirety – has been described on an online perfume retail web site thusly: "An animalic, musky, sensuous odor with costus-like connotation. Can be described as unwashed human hair, goat smell and dirty socks."[30]

Amic approved of this beauty-and-the-beast amalgam, so he passed on the compounded juice to Chantal Roos, the YSL fragrance developer, who asked, Who *made* this? Amic's answer was the first time she'd ever heard the name "Pierre Bourdon." And Roos knew then – I have to meet this perfumer. This is the creator with whom I must work.

It seemed almost like destiny to Pierre: "This was how I met her for the first time, without doubting that she would later be the fairy godmother of my career."

Roos took to the animalic notes in the juice – to the sweaty and uncouth aspect that evoked post-coital funk. So each time Roos requested a mod, no matter what verbiage she used, Bourdon simply increased the dose of carnal chemicals.

Bourdon was not merely playing to his audience here. In April 1977, Amic called Bourdon up to his office – a rare move – and asked him to spend some time with the sister of a friend of Amic's – to talk to a 19-year-old girl considering a career in perfumery about the nature of his work. Which Bourdon did, all the while transfixed by the girl's extraordinary beauty.

Her name was Kathleen Cadore – "Kathy" to her more intimate relations – and she was half-British – had studied in a Trinitarian convent in Kent from the age of 9-18, in fact. Back then, when the young woman had left campus to enter the village, she had to wear the most ridiculous (to her present mind) blazer and straw boater hat.

She was rather devout as a child – her favorite saint remains Saint Anthony – but her desire to be a nun didn't survive her pubescent discovery of boys and parties even though her matriculation at the nunnery did. However, it was clear to Pierre that this schooling had accrued to Kathy's advantage, which was already considerable relative to other women, in his view.

Those manners and ideas she'd obtained while studying across the Channel; the modest, becoming way she smiled (never fulsomely, always attentive to the dictates of the moment); her gentle and kind disposition – all of these appealing, they made her damn near undeniable when allied to those looks, to the first impression men formed based on her physiology alone (however superficial that might be).

But she was a neophyte still, a kid, her schooling in this field not even yet begun. Pierre was merely her guide for two weeks, an interlude that perhaps hinted at what life beside her might entail but was far too short for Pierre to get to know her as deeply as he desired.

Kathy was shipped down to the company's perfumery school in Grasse. For two years, Pierre worked on his creations, this woman who'd seized his imagination miles away, a world apart on the Riviera. It was possible she'd never come back to Paris. Or she'd come back but work for another perfumery conern. Or some other unforeseen twist would render the end of the two years unfairly distant – psychologically, professional, emotionally – from their start.

And then she returned – the year was 1980. Kathy was considered skillful enough to share an office with future star Michel Almairac, who'd go on to create (or co-create) Chopard Heaven, Gucci Pour Homme, Zino Davidoff and Dior Fahrenheit.

Yet for all Almairac would do in the world of perfumery, his office-mate had by far the greater immediate impact on the trade. For Pierre had begun to daydream about Kathy – to lose himself in reveries whose sole object was the radiant, young formulator from the UK.

These distractions, occurring ever more frequently, would become impossible for Pierre to ignore – that was inevitable. As it happened, Pierre was on a train bound for the south of France on a July day, headed for holiday in Grasse, the sunlight pouring into the car, when he could no longer escape the import of these fancies.

I'm in love with her, he realized.

And so Pierre courted her, however brazen such a move was in an office that also was occupied by his wife. It was not long before the woman who'd moved into a room with Almairac was Bourdon's mistress. And not long after that, the lover for whom Bourdon left his wife and daughter, just before Christmas, as part of a typically French love triangle – Bourdon, his wife, and mistress all occupying the same building every day, in spite of the torrid activities attendant to each night.

The messy affair didn't wear on Bourdon so much as invigorate him. "I have fond memories of this turmoil during which I created Kouros," he told me. Bourdon was so giddy, in fact, he actually wore a Walkman, a device just invented in 1979, in the office, so that he could listen to the symphonies of Gustav Mahler, then his favorite composer, while working on his formula.

"Love makes you receptive to music," he said to me.

It was up to Jean Amic, then, to figure out how to maintain peace at Roure despite the dynamics between his talents – a task he had long understood to be central to his CEO role, perfumery being a sensuous – and, again, very French – realm.

In fact, at that very same moment, Bourdon's YSL handler and guide, the aforementioned Chantal Roos, was falling hard for the man who'd become her husband.

In this way, Bourdon's upping the animalic aspects of the new male fragrance with each new mod was neither patronizing nor exploitative but an organic extension of what was going on in its creators' lives beyond the lab: *Body heat.*

Or as Bourdon told me: "It was thus that two lovers conceived a scorching scent, bordering on the smell of a beast."

The final result was a an '80s powerhouse potion marked by its quantity of civet – a no-longer used excretion from the anal gland of that eponymous animal, once used in perfumery both for its element of stank as well as its ability to enhance the potency of other ingredients (such enriching components are sometimes called "exalting agents").

YSL named the fragrance "Kouros" and marketed it as "the scent of living gods." And my, how it polarized opinion, among both creators and consumers, upon its 1981 release.

I asked a former Roure colleague of Pierre's what he thought of it. "Kouros? I do not like. Rude, powerful, macho. A tank top EDT !!" was the emailed reply, the two exclamation points his, not mine.

Pierre himself: "I have never worn Kouros, whose strong identity lacks nuance and refinement, except to test it on me during its development."

And yet, one man close to Pierre did adopt Kouros, without ever explaining to the budding perfumer why he liked it or what this choice of scent signified.

"My father sometimes used it, to my astonishment," Pierre says. "It was, perhaps, for him a roundabout way of paying me a compliment, when he never did directly."

You want to understand the power of perfume? Here was one born of lust – unrestrained luridness – subsequently used by a somewhat cold and distant father to express a warmth he simply couldn't put into words (seemingly).

Kouros: both a consequence of copulation and a wordless code of filial tenderness.

Kouros: an expression of urges originating from the lower brain, or what we feel intensely before we understand ourselves.

Unfortunately, the general public didn't initially find the scent so meaningful or alluring – potential buyers were of the same mind as the perfumer who'd labored to create it – *This is not for us.*

That all changed when Chantal Roos had the maverick idea to sponsor a professional endurance racing team named after the YSL scent and branded everywhere with its mark the drivers' helmets, the autos' bonnets, the racing suits.

Backed by Mercedes-Benz, and powered by its V8, the Kouros team competed in seven races of the 1986 World Sportscar Championship, including Spa Francorchamps in Belgium, Monza in Itality, Silverstone in England, Le Mans in France – all legendary motoring venues.

And at the Nurburgring, perhaps most prestigious of all to the German engineers powering the vehicle, the Kouros team actually won – after which Kouros sales rose as if driven themselves by a Daimler dynamo.

It would be the first in a long list of tremendous successes in the career of Bourdon, including Davidoff Cool Water, 1988, the first real aquatic; Feminite du Bois, 1992, considered the first woody women's scent; Joop! Homme, 1989, the first masculine built around powdery sweetness; and a series of forward-looking masculines constructed with a pineapple top-note, which would become en vogue in 2010, years after Bourdon first propounded the idea.

But this long run, which would ultimately yield Bourdon consideration as the best perfumer of his generation, began with YSL Kouros, in 1981.

Alternatively, one could say it began with the launch of Kouros, even if the scent didn't fully catch on until the racing team began carving up European tracks. And this beginning somehow set a template for future Bourdon releases: As he later seemed perpetually unable to bask in the glory and success of his work, so too was he not to be found celebrating here – although this time his absence was literal and unrelated to psychology, so far as he recalls.

His boss Jean Amic, realizing the untenability of keeping Bourdon, his mistress and his wife in the same office, had transferred the first two to Roure's American office, in Teaneck, New Jersey.

Bourdon, in fact, doesn't recall hearing about the much-publicized

Kouros launch party, which was even described in detail in a nationally-syndicated US newspaper column (Yves Saint Laurent flew in the fast crowd from around the world, staged three ballets for them and then hosted a dinner at the world's most famous eatery at a cost of $200,000).[31] If Pierre was apprised of the 1981 fete, he cared not enough to commit its details to memory.

That was unlikely the case for the man whose family tailoring shop at 7 Rue Royale abutted the site of the party, Maxim's, at 3 Rue Royale: Monsieur Olivier Creed.

He couldn't have overlooked the nearby glamour nor its occasion – the launching of a single men's fragrance! – at the end of his undistinguished debut decade in this same trade.

Who was so talented a perfumer that his scent could prompt such a scene? Olivier must have wondered.

That Pierre was nowhere in evidence did not seem to matter to Olivier – perhaps the absence only enhanced the real perfumer's enigmatic aura, his desirability.

Because from that moment on, Olivier sought out Pierre – or, more accurately, his services. He had found the great talent who could make his eponymous brand the world's best perfumery – and himself an artist. Unable to formulate a masterpiece, he had discovered someone who could, someone he believed, for whatever reason, he could subordinate to his will.

He would employ a ghostwriter – but not just any, such as those he likely had already used for his offerings in Lille. No, this would be a man so obviously talented it'd be audacious even to request he hide himself. Insolent even to make the offer. An *attractive* Cyrano.

Now, maybe Creed's eyewitness perch to Bourdon's first feted success was unrelated to his subsequent pursuit of Pierre. It's impossible to know what's in a man's heart when he not only refuses to reveal its true contents but perpetually obscures them.

But if all you ever wanted to become was the person suddenly being celebrated next door, and you soon pursued that figure as though he were an aromatic Mr. Ripley – a man whose life you could convincingly make your own, so that the whole world would consider you the master – would you really expect anyone to believe such a sequence coincidence?

Yves Saint Laurent and Zizi Jeanmaire at the Kouros launch party
(courtery of Bernard Laforet/Getty Images)

THE GHOST PERFUMER

Chapter 5: Exile

When Pierre Bourdon arrived in America with his partner, Kathy, in the early 1980s, he had no idea what would become of his career or creations. He'd had one major success with a French brand – Kouros for Yves Saint Laurent – but the American market had its own aromatic imperatives and demands:

The release in 1953 of Estee Lauder's powerful Youth-Dew announced that American women liked their scents strong, though contemporary French perfumers used more disparaging terms – their general thought: *Only a night walker, in need of street-level attention to make money, requires such a far-reaching, aggressive aroma.*

Later, the American market was said to have pioneered the top-note. Whereas French perfumes had always unfolded themselves on the skin over a period of hours, their best attributes often unavailable upon application – French shoppers being patient enough to wait for the drydown – Americans apparently demanded a hedonic scent from that first sprayed burst – and bought bottles accordingly. If an initial fruity or citric or minty note was lacking, they'd move on to another counter, without considering how an odor might evolve over ensuing hours.

The rise of unisex, minimalist aquatic fragrances in the '90s is also often credited to Americans, specifically to CK One. These were perfumes for the American who didn't want to wear any – musky, transparent, scented to work in harmony with the skin's natural effusions instead of above or alongside them.

In truth, many of these ideas about American scent trends were exaggerations or easy stereotypes, unreflective of a US market that post-dated France's but had matured far faster than the French wanted to admit.

So, the early 1980s. Pierre Bourdon arrived in a new land – America – he'd been told possessed very different ideas about perfumery than those he valued. Moreover, he was not even relocated to the global capital that is New York City, to a cosmopolitan place that might prize his French accent and manner.

See, in 1972, a 28-year-old rising architect, a Yale alum, had designed for Roure its fine fragrance headquarters in Teaneck, New Jersey – a small town on the wrong side of the Hudson River, just past the George Washington Bridge, north of Route 4 (and the longtime home of my grandfather whom I miss dearly whenever I consider the place).

This architect was named Der Scutt, and a decade later, when Pierre Bourdon was first entering the Roure building in Jersey, Scutt was completing a new structure in Midtown Manhattan, on Fifth Avenue, near the Park: Trump Tower.

Pierre Bourdon, loner, lover of French literature, acolyte of Master Nose Edmond Roudnitska – he wasn't in Kansas (read: Continental Europe) anymore.

And yet, he and Kathy made do: They lived in a West New York apartment with a breathtaking view of the City skyline. Pierre successfully produced a few fragrances for the US market. He got into German literature, which had eluded him for whatever reason when he lived next-door in France, and took pleasure in the novels of Herman Hesse and Thomas Mann.

"My career in this country seemed secure," he told me.

Only the perfume world is not so exotic and libertine that it operates entirely at a remove from domestic matters. Pierre had pursued unyieldingly the goals encouraged implicitly and explicitly during his formative years – by charismatic teachers, lauded literature, indiscreet and ubiquitous French adultery – to become a great artist, to make love to those women who most excited him, regardless of their nuptial status or his own. A hybrid philosophy calling for the examination of life but also its *carpe diem* confiscation.

Yet housed in a slick glass flat atop the basalt bluffs of the Palisades, his view of the Hudson River and Midtown Manhattan commanding and majestic, Pierre nevertheless found himself heavy-hearted and homesick.

He had left behind with his estranged wife a daughter. Pierre was a man whose father was almost never encouraging, yet that very fact implied the father's constant presence. Pierre realized he couldn't even meet that low standard. And he wasn't just out of the house but across the Atlantic Ocean from his daughter.

And then there was France itself. Pierre wasn't an especially patriotic man in the traditional sense – he never fought for his country or ran for office. By the same token, he'd seen his father, orphaned by war and suicide, impoverished and without advantage, nevertheless find his way to the top level of perfume production at Dior.

This was all the proof Pierre needed to believe his nation afforded legitimate social mobility – and the reason Pierre bristled at the student protests of May 1968, which he considered "a fruitless and baseless rebellion."

It was now almost 15 years later, and somehow, Pierre was no longer a part of a France he'd so highly valued and defended – he wasn't creating within its borders, not contributing in any direct way to the cultural capital of the place.

Nor was he enjoying its rewards: its long literary legacy of Balzac,

Zola and Proust, while appreciable anywhere, was more remote when you were no longer traversing the same streets they once had. And the more immediate material benefits – the food, wine, France's overall joie de vivre – were not to be found in Teaneck (nor anywhere else in Bergen County).

Pierre considered repatriating with Kathy, but the issue that prompted his departure remained: The wife from whom he was separated (not amicably) still worked in Roure's Paris office (technically, it was in Argenteuil, just northwest of Paris proper).

Pierre and Kathy couldn't endure that workplace dynamic again – which meant if they were to return to France, they'd need to find a new employer – and leave Roure, the greatest assemblage of olfactive talent in the world.

After only a year or so, Pierre resolved to return and set out on a most bittersweet job search.

There was no denying that he would have to make a tremendous career sacrifice to return to his country and reenter his daughter's life – he and Kathy understood what they were attempting – but that setback was especially underlined by the man who eventually brought them aboard.

His name was John Roberts, and he had led the fragrance company Naarden back when the YSL Kouros competition was ongoing – reaching the finals with his perfumer's entry, finding himself pitted against a then-unknown Pierre Bourdon, who, of course, won.

Now, to get back to France, Pierre had to take a job beneath the fragrance exec whom he'd beaten and consigned to second-place – a kind of poetic underscoring of the challenge he'd face to reestablish himself. And as if the universe were out to humble Pierre (perhaps deservedly), Pierre knew he was not even Robert's first choice for the position – Roberts had recruited Francoise, Pierre's estranged wife, but she'd declined to leave Roure.

There's a reason she didn't jump companies, beyond Roure's excellent reputation and resources. No longer at Naarden, Roberts was now the head of US operations for the Japanese fragrance firm Takasago. To this day, Takasago is seen as an also-ran in perfumery – it receives briefs from minor brands – but back then, it had the added baggage of being known for rank unoriginality – namely, for producing clones of other companies' work exclusively, instead of as a complement to juices of their own invention (which is what the major firms – Givaudan, Firmenich, IFF – offer clients).

Now this Japanese outsider outfit wanted to open up a Paris office and lab, employ creative perfumers therein and challenge the other multinationals for the most prestigious of briefs. Though John Roberts ran Takasago's US business, he was nevertheless the man tasked with finding a head for the Paris office.

Along with a Swedish perfume salesman, Pierre was appointed just that – head of the operation – as well as chief perfumer. Their remit to build the enterprise from scratch, Pierre understood how much labor that would require but found himself exponentially more enervated and anxious than expected once he actually began.

"Arrived in Paris, the task that awaited me was considerable: Wulff and I had to find offices, equip a laboratory there, find perfumers, canvass clients who would agree to work with a Japanese company at a time when the Japanese had the reputation of only making copies," Bourdon emailed me. "I quickly realized that I had taken an inordinate risk."

Pierre also wasn't quite so liberated from corporate bureaucracy as his assignment implied: Yes, Takasago wanted to build a brand new operation but it wasn't entirely without a forebear. Decades earlier, the Japanese company had made its first tentative moves in Paris, and one man from that operation remained in the new one, to serve as the eyes of the executives back in Tokyo.

But Pierre never did clash with Mr. Yamada, his Orwellian Big Brother – in fact, bizarrely, the most significant moment involving the Japanese executive installed in Paris saw him not as powerful overseer but submissive victim:

In the summer of 1984, an Air France flight from Frankfurt to Paris was hijacked and flown to Tehran, the Iranian terrorists demanding the release of five compatriots then imprisoned in France. Amazingly, all 63 people on board ultimately made it through the 48-hour ordeal physically unharmed; the terrorists wound up turning them over to authorities, having realized France had no intent of freeing prisoners, and then blowing up the empty Boeing 737 they'd so chillingly commandeered days earlier.

The whole episode had a cinematic quality, but Pierre's superior played perhaps the most obvious of disaster flick roles: That unlucky foreigner, who, because of a petty corporate decision made a million miles away, winds up ensnared in a potentially fatal international intrigue.

Indeed, Yamada-san, the Takasago man the company had *intentionally left behind* – just to have one Japanese person peering over Pierre's soldier – was a passenger on that ill-fated Air France flight, and then a captive on the plane once it was parked.

That Yamada made it back alive, if shaken, allows us to return without seeming too cold to just that beauty venture that had put his future in jeopardy, his fate at the mercy of pirates.

So…Pierre and the Swede, Wolff, acquired and furnished an office on Avenue George V, neither move allaying Bourdon's doubts that he'd made a terrible mistake in departing Roure for Takasago.

Always wily, Jean Amic got in touch with Pierre and told him he was doomed if he stayed at Takasago, that Pierre wasn't yet renowned enough to be briefed by major firms by virtue of his reputation alone, so he'd never win any big competitions. *Come back to Roure*, Amic concluded. *You can become a star here. Of course, you can't bring Kathy...* This last bit made Amic's otherwise reasonable proposal a non-starter. It didn't help Amic's case either that he was a terribly miserly boss, according to Pierre. Nearly every excellent perfumer he ever had left for a job elsewhere – often at a worse company – simply because Amic refused to pay the going rate for the perfumer's services.

Amic's sincere belief was that perfumers were far more replaceable than olfactive auteur theory – that individual geniuses are the engines of the industry – would have you believe. He was the Billy Beane of perfumery long before there was one of baseball – before a statistics-minded former ballplayer staffed the Oakland Athletics with unknowns, declining to pay big stars and instead compensating for their lost production with a coterie of lesser overall players who nevertheless each had a single strong suit and could collectively increase wins.

Takasago, meanwhile, went big time to ensure Pierre stayed put in their fledgling fine fragrance office, offering him *twice* the salary proposed by Amic plus 3 percent of the Paris office's revenue. Kathy could work in the office – in the absence of the wife, the lover was perfectly welcome – and thus entrenched again in Paris, handsomely paid, the couple rented a two-bedroom apartment Kathy had found on the Rue de Beaux Arts in Saint-Germain-des-Prés.

Somehow, from a perch atop a brand new office of a poorly-perceived foreign company, Pierre began to thrive. Yves Saint Laurent awarded Pierre the YSL skincare line (yes, these products are perfumed, too) and L'Oréal briefed Pierre on upcoming projects, despite his being a small operation.

This acceptance by the beauty world, in fact, led Michel Almairac, a highly-skilled perfumer and one of Bourdon's few true friends, a man he considered his brother, to join the Takasago office – which could now boast of having two stars instead of just one.

It was true, as Amic had said with an ulterior motive, that Pierre wasn't receiving the most prestigious briefs in the business and was therefore being denied with each such project a chance to show the world what he could do, to make his mark.

But business was good. Pierre began collecting antiques with some of his expendable income. At night, Pierre and Kathy would dine at Lipp, Voltaire or Tsukisi, on Rue des Ciseaux, or Chez Bartolo, on Rue de Canettes, and later, when they opened, Atelier de Joël Robuchon and Gaya Rive Gauche.

Of course, neither Pierre nor Kathy nor Michel– nobody in the picture would have suspected that such a bright period might blind our main character to an otherwise avoidable trap. Or that his acceptance by the perfume establishment that could have easily dismissed his entire office would open the door also to a shifty man named Olivier Creed.

Chapter 6: Faustus

The late '70s and early '80s were not a distinguished period for Olivier Creed. He has told publications he shuttered the men's clothing store at 7 Rue Royale in 1970. But that's not true – he continued running ads for his tailoring service there as late as 1978.

In the June 20, 1974, edition of Le Monde Diplomatique, Olivier told customers they could choose their own fabrics from his exclusive English collections. In August in the same paper, his ad ran nearby one for a Peugeot Sodexo. In 1978, one Creed ad proclaimed "special discount – January 10%."

Oh, and the Creed slogan printed in the ad: *"Tailleur depuis 1760,"* or "Tailor since 1760."

There's nothing dishonorable in being a garment worker, no matter your station or wealth. The ads and their subsequent deletion from Olivier's personal narrative speak to *his* own shame of his profession and past, though, as well as its general dullness, and the decline of bespoke suit tailoring as a service altogether.

Add in the fact that Olivier Creed had never wanted to run his predecessors' haberdashery and that his first attempts at perfumery made no impression and you have a man unhappy with his professional lot in life in this period.

While Pierre Bourdon was standing on a craggy cliff in New Jersey watching the Hudson River drift by, skyscrapers glinting in the background, a perfumer who fled his homeland with his mistress pondering a return, Olivier was seeking the best possible perfumers for his nascent fragrance operation in the absence of the contemplative master.

Where Olivier got the idea, let alone the temerity, I don't know but in this period, Creed began walking in unannounced into perfumers' offices. So far, his eponymous line of fragrances had failed to make an impression. Smart enough to understand where superior scents could be found, the man literally began making uninvited visits to perfumers' offices and sniffing all the vials of scents-in-development lying on desks, tables and shelves (and if you've ever visited the office of a perfumer, you know there are always a million mods all over the place – a mod being a twist or variation of a perfume-in-development).

Technically, he had no right to be in these places – and certainly not to assess the confidential work. But Olivier Creed had three attributes that allowed him to get away with it regardless: he knew how to target the vulnerable; he was brilliant at evaluating their works, at determining which would best reflect on Creed as the ostensible maker; and he had the cash to make such a transfer of credit – a revision of history – possible.

Listen to the story of perfumer Bernard Ellena – from the same part of Southern France where Bourdon learned with Roudnitska – on how Creed somehow acquired one of his perfumes, which Olivier released as "Acier Aluminium" and dated to 1973:

"I was a young perfumer, and I was working on several olfactory tracks to learn my profession. Olivier Creed used to come improvised into my office, and he could smell everything that was lying around. That's how he found 'Acier Aluminium.'"

I can't help but find this encounter a creepy violation, besides an obvious trespass. Sure, Ellena yields the fragrance ultimately in a deal he wouldn't disclose. But the perfumer here is still a novitiate, working hard to improve, worried about all the little things a perfumer must get right for each formula to work. And then an older man with a big checkbook walks in, smells vials reflective of a perfumer's intimate notions, accords developed over years of perfumery school and apprenticeship, and offers to buy a scent off a kid who doesn't yet know the value of his own work.

And none of that addresses the most problematic hypothetical: If it really is good juice and market-ready, no one will think more of Ellena for it because he has just sold away the right to claim it as his own – at a stage of his career when such credits are crucial to elevation. Will his role be leaked or become an open industry secret? It could have. But 40 years later, I can say, It didn't. Nobody knows.

Creed burns attempted not to underscore Ellena's role but cover it up. Here's the company's story of the creation:

"Inspired by the armor of interlocking metal (known as 'chain mail') worn by knights in the Middle Ages, Acier Aluminium makes a daring statement of unmistakably masculine strength and power."

Acier Aluminium, despite the above crusader nonsense, was never a hit, so Creed next went after Bourdon's estranged wife, perfumer Francoise Cresp. One would think this a rather ingenious pick on the part of Olivier, as Francoise had always been known in the industry as too self-effacing for her own good, too eager to attribute the success of her work to those around her (including to Pierre Bourdon himself when they were still living together).

If Ellena was too young to say anything about Olivier's sneakiness, Francoise would be too down on herself to try. Her husband ran off with a beautiful young woman, after all – and she'd been diffident to start. Colleague Raymond Chaillan of Roure described Francoise thusly to me: "First impression not great, second impression not better!

Still tearful in my office, uneasy about being an on-board perfumer."

But unexpectedly, Francoise's great discomfort during Olivier's office intrusion didn't precede meek acquiescence. Rather, she had enough wits about her to get rid of him and get back at her ex simultaneously: She sent Olivier Creed to a new office on Avenue George V – the Parisian headquarters of Japanese fragrance company Takasago.

(Although that was likely just the proximate reason for Olivier's first visit to Pierre – because if Olivier knew the industry as he claimed, he was well-aware of Pierre by this point, had taken notice of the Kouros launch party next door to his own store and the huge sum the Japanese had paid Pierre to be its European leader – and the potential problem inherent in such a free agent move: Pierre would soon receive fewer big briefs, meaning he would *have* to concentrate on making money off the little guys, by hook or crook, in some sense. Another indication he was out to snag Bourdon from the start: the way he stuck with Pierre for the ensuing *three* decades. Perhaps he wended his way through Pierre's associates first as if to put out feelers, see what behaviors would and would not fly.)

When Olivier did finally show up at Pierre's door, Bourdon was working on submissions for a L'Oréal brief – one that called for a feminine scent inspired by jazz, by that music's blue notes. (Indeed, when the product came to market in 1983, it was called "Courreges in Blue"; L'Oréal had licensed the fashion brand of space-age designer Andre Courreges, known for his use of PVC and nylon in the service of big, bright geometric forms.)

Olivier entered without invitation, sat at Bourdon's desk and began uncorking all the bottles lying around, questioning Bourdon about their eventual recipients but not their contents. Strange, that.

Pierre did not recall for me whether Olivier out-and-out asked him to be his ghostwriter during that first meeting or whether it was discussed over the many more meetings that followed.

"Since we had offices a stone's throw from his shop, he kept coming to see me unexpectedly," Bourdon recalls of his first encounters with Olivier. "He was intrusive and I dreaded his forays."

What lay at the center of that dread, beyond Olivier's utter disregard of convention and propriety, his aggressive manner? And if Bourdon hated the visits so much, why didn't he make a stronger effort to end them, cut Olivier off?

On the evidence, I'd wager Olivier had found in Bourdon the weakness he knew he could exploit: It was Pierre's relationship with his father and what it had done to his willpower.

During the 1980s, past the point of Pierre's Kouros success, Pierre was still sending works in development to his father to get the older man's evaluation (despite the father having worked *with* perfumers but never as one himself – unlike the son – and the foregone conclusion that the father would eviscerate the son no matter his merits).

From a typewritten 1984 letter from Rene to Pierre on a batch of scents:

My Dear Pierre,

A little meditation before sending you this note...You cannot continue in the current way if what you sent me is representative of your work, lest you one day find yourself in front of a formidable deadline, which will be the end of your credibility. We must therefore change the method. See, in any case, here, the words a septuagenarian can make to his soon-to-be forty-year-old son, in a manner of solicitude, exaggerated but surely affectionate.

Nothing emerges in the products you gave me. The twist can be seen sometimes but it remains too little for me...Do not take account of this mediocrity – let's say, rather, insufficiency – by taking a step back...You don't need salespeople but better products.

This father-son inferiority complex that beset Pierre – this was his vulnerability — and it was no minor one either. Every time

Bourdon lost a brief, it was as though his father's cruel opinions had been validated. And so rather than deal in the reworking of failed scents, Pierre was sometimes eager to let them go, if only to ignore the accuracy of his father's withering assessments.

Olivier likely could sense Pierre's fraught relationship to those scents he'd lost and was primed to take advantage of just such a complex, perhaps with sweet-talk along these lines:

Look, if this work doesn't win the brief, please don't discard it – not only is it not trash, I wanna share it with the public after all – just under my name. Still, you won't have to change anything – your work is brilliant as is. I might sub in some more expensive alternative ingredients, naturals and things, captives from Firmenich that the company permits me to use. But your work is structurally brilliant. Those who say otherwise are simply wrong.

In the moment, Pierre, by his own later admission, didn't quite understand he was being sweet-talked by someone who understood the perfumer's self-doubt and whose price was actually the selling of Pierre's soul.

In fact, Pierre was so taken by this suave and deep-pocketed charmer, his looks a cross between Sean Connery's and Roger Moore's, not to mention that he was so bereft each time a formula of his was shot down, he agreed to terms so ludicrous as to make one wonder whether Pierre wasn't the more culpable party in the affair.

A deal that invites you to blame the victim – as a grown man besotted, clueless while trying to act cool.

Olivier literally called Pierre his "best friend" during the brokering of the deal, promised Pierre that he'd make him a couple of custom suits for each formula handed over and added that he'd pay Pierre a handsome sum upon the perfumer's retirement — a bounty whose size Pierre disclosed to me on several occasions before suddenly requesting, just weeks prior to this book's printing, that I not share the figure and run the following disclaimer in its place:

He — Pierre — had never really felt he was *owed* this pledged money, as Olivier's promise was less a formal commitment than the casual, non-binding oath of an old pal, the sort of offer whose later unfulfillment is not among chums considered reneging.

And surely, that line was crafted from the heart by Pierre, his sudden reticence and legalese — the subversion of a story he'd told me countless times in the prior months — based not in fear of being sued unjustly for defamation by a man capable of paying far more in legal fees but in a sincere re-remembrance of how events *actually* unfolded.

That was it – the sum total of Olivier's remuneration offer — suits and a fat check the now-septuagenarian can't yet bring himself to detail in writing.

Bourdon – brilliant student of literature, observer of humanity's mistakes while blind to his own – accepted the deal. It was and will likely forever remain the most lopsided agreement ever struck in the beauty industry. A case of a spurned middle school boy doing the cool kid's homework for no reward greater than a (fleeting) feeling of acceptance.

Pierre's emailed recollection of how things went down thereafter:

"He used a simple method: by dint of pulling the worms out of my nose to find out what projects I was in the final on, he waited for me to lose them and, like a scavenger, [pounced upon] my formulas."

(It should be added that Pierre wasn't uniquely influenced by parental opinion in the perfume game. "I was wondering If the father syndrome/complex was not a common thread throughout all the perfumers," former Firmenich master Harry Fremont, creator of Aramis New West and Tom Ford Grey Vetiver, emailed me a couple months after I visited his home in 2021. "I do believe the father syndrome can be positive (it was for me) or negative. This is universal for humankind, but when I look around at the perfumers I know, I think it is quite a potent force influencing each perfumer's character and will to succeed in this difficult business.")

Olivier Creed's first acquisition? Pierre's submission for the Courrèges in Blue project,[32] which wound up losing to Edouard Fléchier of Roure – Pierre's old firm, the one whose head, Jean Amic, had asked Pierre to return but also deemed him overpaid and replaceable when Pierre rebuffed him.

Was Pierre, in fact, replaceable? Fléchier had just beaten him out, after all. And in two years, Fléchier would create Poison for Dior – the only brand whose work Pierre's father could never dismiss. The only company whose output mattered in that strange Bourdon domicile. Could Pierre have been its author had only he stayed at Roure, never taken on a lover and found himself banished?

Was the door to Dior forever closed now instead?

Of course, there was another way of looking at the above sequence – which just so happened to benefit Olivier Creed's commercial ambition. Fléchier had beaten out Bourdon on Courreges, sure – but only because L'Oréal said so. In other words: The judgment was subjective. Perhaps L'Oréal was wrong and Creed, now the owner of the formula, right. Bourdon's stuff was fantastic – any evaluator who failed to realize it didn't deserve the title.

This line of thinking would be attractive to the loser of any subjective contest but was especially so to Pierre, who had always been both stubborn and insecure and his father's boy.

Did he want his scents out in the world? Yes, he believed them worthy of that honor. Did he want to spend time altering them so that could reach the market, reexamine them such that he'd have to recall his father's assessments? Hardly.

And so a perfume produced to win a L'Oréal brief – of the sort Pierre once believed his new company's salvation – became a Creed fragrance – was bought from the losing perfumer, a man generally hardheaded, at his most vulnerable moment.

Olivier Creed called it Fleurs de Bulgarie, a harmless enough name for a floral scent: Flowers of Bulgaria.

But then Olivier released an origin story to the media, a narrative of how and when this perfume came to be – the first real indication Pierre had agreed to far more than he'd realized in exchange for the self-affirming, daddy-complex-induced release of his rejected efforts.

"Creed Fleurs de Bulgarie was originally created in 1845 for Queen Victoria, under whose reign Creed served as an official supplier to the royal court...."

Chapter 7: The King

King Alfonso XIII of Spain was a sad little sovereign. In the early 20th century, before Generalissimo Francisco Franco ruled that country, this king of French descent evangelized for rule by dictatorship – until, in 1931, the Spanish people demanded a proper republic.

At which point King Alfonso, outflanked by these constituents, outfoxed by their liberal ideals, fled.

A UPI bulletin, April 15, 1931:

"Last night the king, who had tried to be an 'iron monarch' and failed, then tried to be a small-town politician and failed, slipped from the royal palace, fearful of an attempt on his life. He took one of his racing cars and left Madrid. He was accompanied only by his chauffeur and two other autos bearing attendants.

"For seven hours the deposed monarch sped across Spain, thru towns and cities where 'viva la republica' was heard on every hand…Few in Madrid knew he had left until hours afterward. At 4 a.m. the three autos swung into the dockyards at Cartagena.

"A few officials were waiting at the pier with a motorboat. Alfonso greeted them and stepped into the boat. Then he turned back to those on shore.

"I preserve and follow my traditions. 'Viva Espana!' he said.

"'Viva la republica' came back from the small group."

Thusly rejected even in valediction, the failed king sailed away, only to die 10 years later in 1941, as Europe convulsed from World War II.[33]

Why anyone would want to resurrect a monarch so pathetically deposed is a mystery. Nevertheless, Creed told Forbes in 1999 that its perfumery had created the scent Green Irish Tweed for this impotent nonentity. [34]

The actual scent was like a still from a movie – a snapshot of a single moment in a years-long Pierre Bourdon project.

It began again with a brief from Elisabeth Carles of L'Oréal – this time for the fragrance that would become Lancome Sagamore, a sandalwood-lavender masculine of 1986 now almost entirely forgotten.[35]

The winner was again a Roure hand – Jean-Louis Sieuzac, emphasizing once more to Pierre that he'd left the company whose power would help him make history, win all the briefs, leave behind a substantial record of his existence on this orb.

The episode also underscored the traditionalism of the very institutions Pierre was querying – and pushing – such that success there perhaps no longer seemed much of a compliment. Was he even in the proper profession? Pierre had an idea in mind – one so much bigger than a formula occasioned by any one particular L'Oréal query.

So Elisabeth Carles asked for Sagamore submissions and she chose as her winner the spicy-woody by Roure's Jean-Louis Sieuzac, Bourdon's one-time colleague. But while they didn't see it then, even Carles and Sieuzac acknowledge now a short-sightedness at the time.

Carles: "The note of Sieuzac had a very 'French man' charm. The modernity of Pierre Bourdon's note and its potential were not understood."

Sieuzac on Sagamore: "A flop. The market had just changed.

Everything was too classic – marketing, the bottle and the perfume...

"A posteriori, Pierre must have been delighted not to win it because if I am not mistaken his reworked submission has become Cool Water... What a success!"

Sieuzac is half-right. Pierre had a big idea in mind, one that remains in two hugely sought-after scents 35 years later. But the first is not Davidoff Cool Water at all, but a Creed fragrance of Olivier's co-opting. And Pierre has never appreciated losing – it's just these losses, allied with paternal pressure, made him yield works of genius to a serial perjurer.

"When I lost the finale of Lancôme's Sagamore project," Bourdon recalls of his next run-in with Olivier, "he stole my formula from me, modified it to make it his Green Irish Tweed."

Stole: Not literally, of course, but in the sense that Pierre now feels betrayed and robbed, yes. And modified, because Olivier would sometimes take the ingredients Pierre recommended and replace them with the most expensive version of those ingredients or some novel Firmenich-sourced take on the ingredient (Olivier had no idea how to meet a perfume's budget; this resulted in luxurious products but he couldn't have cut costs even if he'd wanted to, according to a source).

Stole: Because the scent Creed told Forbes was made for King Alfonso XIII – that most bizarre historical faux-inspirational figure – was another runner-up entry by Bourdon – but more importantly, his first take on an idea that had been germinating inside him essentially since he'd finished the sex-stanky Kouros.

The 1980s had proceeded apace ever since that scent's 1981 release, and aside from the era's speed and greed, it was marked by a kind of dynamic watery-green machismo. In 1982, an IFF perfumer had created Drakkar Noir, whose greenery – basil, artemisia, mint, fir and moss – possessed an almost ethereal airiness – a kind of aquatic-adjacent coolness – an effect later termed "ozonic" in industry parlance

– owed to the use of dihydromyrcenol.

The following year brought another IFF-created novelty to the market in the women's YSL Paris, whose damascone – a fruity-rose-green note – had only just begun to be incorporated into perfumery, having been synthesized commercially on a wider scale only the prior decade. Damascones are related to ionones, as well – the chemical underpinning of a violet note in a fragrance, a note prominent in Geoffrey Beene's Grey Flannel of 1975.

For Bourdon, this history was none of it piecemeal or without implication. He envisioned in the mid-1980s an ethereal clubby-green-violet ideal – a scent as refreshing and rejuvenating as his Kouros had been sweaty and heated.

The mark of great olfactive ambition: to produce a classic entirely unlike your prior one, a diametrically opposite odor – but not just for the sake of innovation but to fit the era – to define it.

His submission for Lancome Sagamore, coming as it did in the middle of the decade, was merely then the first shot he took at achieving the perfect balance of these elements – at attaining the equipoise inherent to a classic scent, one that can stay decades on the market without ever becoming stale or passe.

To the degree Creed filched it, he took an idea under development. Here's how Pierre described his failed Sagamore submission – ie the underpinnings of Green Irish Tweed – in an emailed essay to me:

"My submission was a Drakkar Noir whose innovations I had multiplied tenfold, namely dihydromyrcenol (multiplied by four), ambroxan (X 5), allyl amyl glycolate and galbex - the pineapple complex (X 4), the triplal (X 5), damascone (X 4) and the orange blossom note. I had grafted onto it a violet accord borrowed from Grey Flannel."

To call the Creed-bought iteration of this dream – Green Irish Tweed – a market success (to borrow a term from Sieuzac) would be a tremendous understatement. The scent came out in 1985. Twenty years later I interned in Esquire's fashion closet, under editor Nick Sullivan, who wore Green Irish Tweed. In 2001, the Dallas Morning News said it was the best-selling men's scent downtown. As in, in downtown Dallas, in Texas, a million miles in space-time-thought from the moments in which it was conceived.[36] An 8.4 oz flacon of the stuff costs $660 at Bloomingdale's at this very moment, in June 2021, in the middle of a pandemic.

Meanwhile, back in the 1980s, Pierre kept modifying his idea and submitting his latest version in response to briefs. Elisabeth Carles of L'Oréal, having rejected the idea for the male Sagamore, accepted it again for the contest to make O de Lancome Intense – a women's scent.

While Carles could not always control who won or lost – she had her own higher-ups and deciders to deal with – she wanted Pierre to remain in the picture, could tell from their conversations he was onto something big:

"Pierre always had a clear, limpid discourse on his vision of a creation," she told me. "He clearly explained the work on dihydromyrcenol to find a 'new freshness'... He is a great perfumer, a true creator, a visionary. I just wanted to try to allow the brands in the group to have access to his masterful creations."

But again Pierre lost, this time to Florence Idier, a woman who'd go on to do three scents for Christian Dior, Pierre's father's company and the son's bete noire. Other assays were submitted to Paco Rabanne for Tenere – lost – Yves Saint Laurent for Jazz – lost – Hermes for Bel Ami – lost.

According to Pierre, he actually won the Tenere brief at first, but the man who chose it – one Monsieur Gomez – was killed in an accident on a mountain and his successor went in a different direction.

And Chantal Roos of YSL told Pierre his submission smelled of "green beans" (I asked her whether she recalls saying this and she didn't choose to confirm or deny it, merely repeating to me instead that no matter how good Pierre's creation was, it was the wrong fit for her Jazz project, never mind that she herself couldn't have cared less about Jazz once a snobby American executive with little understanding of the project changed it from a female scent to a male one).

"When Cool Water became an international success," Pierre adds, "she criticized me for not having reserved this masterpiece for her. She was not lacking in nerve or had a short memory!"

Then there was the final of Bel Ami for Hermes. Pierre recalls being told by Jean-Louis Dumas, the manager of Hermes: "Your perfume has all the qualities of a huge hit. This is why I will not adopt it – too much success in our perfume business risks changing the image of Hermès, which is the essence of our business."

"I was devastated by this rather specious argument!" Pierre tells me.

So devastated, in fact, that Pierre returned tail-between-the-legs to his old Roure boss Jean Amic, who was close friends with Dior's CEO, Maurice Roger. Dior was developing a new masculine – Fahrenheit. Could Amic submit Pierre's scent for that brief?

Pierre was someone who'd turned down Amic's offer to return to the company once. Though he made no such larger concession here, Pierre was nevertheless prostrating himself – as if Amic had been right all along, Roure was where Pierre should have stayed, he should never have taken a mistress and allowed his removal to New York. Sure, Pierre had ideas. But ideas alone were worthless. Power flowed from position, from alliances with the already-powerful. Pierre had fucked up.

This was not a statement Pierre made aloud nor was it what he truly believed. But did a part of him believe it? On the evidence of his action alone, one would have to say yes.

But Pierre was also "certain of the value of my perfume." It was this conviction more than anything that led him to implore his old boss.

Not that anything came of it – nobody from Dior ever got back to him. Pierre's current boss was no less confident in the juice – so John Roberts of Takasago submitted the scent to Calvin Klein, which also declined to proceed.

"In all, I had eight refusals," Pierre says. "Tired of my perseverance, one depressed day I almost tore up all the formulas in my assays. Instead, I put them in an envelope and threw it in the bottom of a drawer. I forgot that cursed scent."

Such was Pierre's intense devotion to his craft and commensurate fragility. The man wasn't upset at loss of money or status. He hadn't tailored his scents particularly for each new business opportunity. He developed what he felt was the quintessential perfume of his time. When the world didn't want it – a kind of self-fulfilling prophecy if you never create based on worldly demand in the first place – he couldn't bear any further exposure to the world. He was his idea. The rejection of his work was a rejection of his being.

In this sense, the world was almost lucky that a sneaky puss like Creed had inserted himself in the middle of this tumultuous period and for a small sum finagled from the lab a version of the scent of the century, of Pierre's dream juice. At least one version, albeit an early one, made it to market as a result – no matter that besides King Alfonso XIII, Creed would later claim as inspiration for the scent (a scent he said he stated was his own creation) Cary Grant, boasting he'd whipped it up for the movie star just before the latter's death (a claim later repeated by Details Magazine, The New York Daily News, The San Francisco Chronicle, and The New Zealand Herald, among others).[37]

Not that Green Irish Tweed is the only iteration of Bourdon's '80s passion project to exist still (and thrive).

After the eight failures, an encounter from Pierre's past – really, his chance appearance at a party he only attended in place of a friend –

redounded to his benefit – redeemed a decade of misfortune.

The Lancaster company of Germany, which licensed the intellectual property of cigar-maker Davidoff, had accepted a submission from Pierre's friend and then-colleague Michel Almairac in the mid-1980s. The perfume was intended to be a masculinized version of Guerlain's Shalimar and remains a striking scent due to that construction to this day – but because Almairac left the company before the big launch party, Pierre had to attend in Almairac's place.

Thusly did Pierre find himself in Salzburg, Austria, in 1986, before a most promising party audience, including Zino Davidoff himself, who'd founded his eponymous firm as a cigar shop in Basel; its current head, Ernst Schneider; and the president of Lancaster, the company tasked with making Davidoff fragrances, Herbert Frommen.

No, none of these men was yet a name in the fragrance world. There was no real prestige attached to their brands either. And though the first Davidoff scent, in 1984, had been handled by Roure, these men – from Germany and Geneva – didn't care about historical pedigree.

In fact, they hardly seemed to care about perfumery at all. And yet, having met Pierre and gotten to know him, they were nevertheless drawn to what he had to offer.

A couple years after that party in Austria, just as Pierre was on the verge of discarding all his papers from the grand ozonic project, a man named Michael Foerster, upon instruction from Lancaster head brass, visited the perturbed perfumer.

"We are contractually bound to launch a third eau de toilette," Foerster said, regarding the license deal with Davidoff. "We're going to do it, although we don't think it will work. You showed me this perfume you've tried to sell so many times, and while it's not the type of note I like, we're going to take it to please you. I warn you that there will only be one order of 500 kilos. Knowing this, if you agree to cede it to us, we will call it Davidoff III."

It could have seemed to Pierre an overly dry – if not offensive – offer, but recall that these were Germans licensing the brand name of a Swiss cigar company: this was perhaps as much enthusiasm as they ever showed a perfumer. Besides, Pierre had been on the verge of discarding all his formulas anyway, of scrapping a near-decade of work.

"It was better than nothing," Pierre recalls. "I took out the formula from the last try."

Of course, the name would soon change – Michael Foerster adopted the moniker "Cool Water" after a trip to California. He further adopted a blue glass bottle evocative of the ocean and marine-themed advertising after watching Luc Besson's 1988 film "The Big Blue."

That the project was a smash is likely already apparent to the reader (who hasn't heard of Cool Water or even seen it being sold in CVS, an unauthorized retailer obsessed with buying up stock on the grey market and reselling it?). But here are some details to that effect, anyway:

Not long after its 1988 release, Cool Water became the best-selling fragrance in Germany. Not long after that, the best-selling scent in the entire world – only France never took to it, which to this day Pierre does not fail to mention (nicked in a winning battle, Pierre meditates on the affliction rather than the outcome – this is his nature, no matter how positive he'd prefer to be).

Cool Water has now been on the market for 32 years. In just the first 16, the fragrances under that brand name – flankers were introduced – generated $1.75 billion in sales. *Billion.*

My high school girlfriend wore Cool Water for Women, which, also Pierre's work, took in $30 million in US sales alone in 2001, my first year of high school.[38]

In 2009, Cool Water was still the fourth best-selling scent overall in England. In 2014, it was still the fourth best-selling men's scent in

Germany by one metric.[39]

But the success of Cool Water can't be measured in numbers alone: it's also credited with inaugurating the '90s trend for fresh and aquatic scents. Without Cool Water, you might never get in the following decade Calvin Klein's Eternity for Men or CK One or Giorgio Armani's Acqua di Gio, among countless other ethereal-marine hits.

Pierre underlined the point for me in an unbecomingly triumphal manner: "I had created a trend and was quite proud of having equaled, if not surpassed, my Master Edmond Roudnitska with his Eau Sauvage."

Where Pierre stands in the hierarchy of perfumer legends is hardly a matter he should state himself. And yet, in so doing, Pierre seemed not to boast of his achievements so much as betray his doubtfulness of their worth. The man's first instinct in discussing his unique creation was to compare it to another – and not just any other perfume either but the one developed at Dior during his adolescence. He literally felt compelled to namecheck the perfumer who worked for Dior and his father, Roudnitska.

A story out-of-time about Pierre: In his retirement, he still writes formulas for perfumes he has no intention of ever actually selling. He also wrote a novel about a perfumer, whom he patterned after Roudnitska, that he has never shown to anyone, save for a single editor who passed on it. Pierre decided the manuscript should never again see the light of day, wary of being wounded further after that single rejection.

When I first contacted him, Pierre said, I guess my career wasn't such a waste, after all.

And so whatever off-putting swagger he displayed in the aftermath of Cool Water's creation was only fractionally egotistical – was much more a product of fearfulness – that he wasn't actually the star he was supposed to be.

In fact, in describing the roller-coaster nature of his career, Pierre quoted the old French saw *"Mais le Capitole est proche de la roche Tarpéienne!"* Or, in other words, the road from present-day power to irrelevancy and ruination is a short one.

But he wasn't about to be ruined yet.

Somehow, Bourdon managed to revolutionize fragrance again, just a year after the Cool Water release, with his Joop! Homme of 1989. He was helped by the ease of the negotiations, the lack of distractions posed by the business side of the affair: Joop! was another Lancaster brand, so he was dealing with the same straightforward Germans who'd overseen Cool Water. There was a mutual understanding and trust now.

As for the actual idea, Bourdon was just in the zone – one could argue that Joop! best represents his philosophy of perfumery – that Kouros and Cool Water, the more well-known hits, are the products of bolts-out-of-the-blue instead of rigorous and painstaking construction (I suppose genius comes in two forms).

That philosophy would be to maintain classical architecture in new perfumes while inserting in the place of expected ingredients novel ones. And so for Zino of 1986, which Michel Almairac created after being influenced by Pierre, Almairac took the structure of feminine classic Guerlain Shalimar – citrus and florals upon a vanilla-tonka base – and masculinized it (sorry for the gendered language, anyone can wear anything, this is just useful shorthand for describing the ideas behind the moves), solidifying the base with cedar, sandalwood and patchouli, while eliminating the tonka. The top was given that classic male barbershop duo of lavender and rosewood in place of Shalimar's florals.

This was classic Bourdon brainstorming – the creation of the new via reverence for the old. Expertise born of historical understanding. And the same process was applied in the Joop! Homme case – only now, the classic ingredients being replaced weren't giving way to bracing or starchy notes but semi-sweet ones.

The scent featured vanilla, cinnamon and heliotrope, whose union was airy and coquettish, never saccharine; a tobacco only slightly tough tempering the above triad's most indulgent aspects; and a classically masculine base of honey and patchouli without the dankness and Burt Reynolds chest hair such a mixture might in lesser hands evoke.

While Joop! Homme launched in December 1989 in Germany, it took a couple of years for it to reach the American market, at which point it became clear how clever the Bourdon juice was. By September 1992, Joop! Homme was a top-five seller in US department stores.[40] For Christmas 1992, Joop! Homme was named a bestseller by Federated Department Stores (ie Macy's and Bloomingdale's), The Parisian and the international perfume chain store Parfumerie Douglas.[41]

It's still on the market and can be found practically everywhere. And its usage of tobacco and honey, of heliotrope, within a certain envelope, with a kind of gentlemanly (and therefore, sexy) restraint, has been echoed in a million scents released since its arrival, including recently Xerjoff Naxos and Psychodelic Love by Initio Parfums, which retail for $250 and $305 per 100 ml, respectively.

For a tenth of those prices, the original thing along with Cool Water occupied together best-seller lists for a decade. Bourdon still found himself a standing capitol, not ruined yet.

Which brings us back to Olivier Creed.

Cool Water being the final version of a scent long under development, its success never imperiled the earlier iteration Olivier had snagged for Creed, Green Irish Tweed. Nor did Creed's shameless tale-telling about the scent's origin – that it was made by him or another Creed family member either for Cary Grant or, alternatively, King Alfonso XIII – hinder Pierre's career – because those eight rejections were followed by an unparalleled promulgation of Pierre's work around the globe. Olivier could tell any story he wanted – no one could diminish the case Cool Water made for Pierre's talent.

But that massive celebration of his ingenuity very nearly hadn't come to pass – Pierre had been days – maybe moments – away from discarding his hand-written Cool Water formulas and notes before Davidoff came barging into his office as the great intercessor and savior. And it was the same folks who gave him another opportunity to shine with Joop! Homme just a year later.

Surely, such a happy last-second save couldn't come to pass in a career again. Bourdon had benefitted from one Deus ex machina and knew well some never even receive that.

And so Pierre had to look in the mirror and ask himself: After a decade of mostly rejection, how many more could he withstand before yielding — in this case, literally yielding his work either to the dust bin or to Olivier for a few bucks? How much more susceptible would he be to the rich man's predation?

The answer would come just a few years later, in the mid-1990s, and involves the story of a king – not Alfonso XIII, who abdicated his throne and fled Spain in a boat in the 1930s but of a similarly controversial commander: King Faisal of Saudi Arabia, who reigned from 1964 to 1975 before being assassinated by his nephew.

In the same Forbes article that stated Creed had devised Green Irish Tweed for King Alfonso, the writer was happy to relay that Creed's Millesime Imperial,[42] a salty-melon scent actually released in 1995, was made for King Faisal of Saudi Arabia (presumably before he was assassinated in the Seventies).[43] The New York Times added: "A Middle Eastern monarch is supposed to have insisted upon a gold bottle to package his own fragrance, Millesime Imperial."[44]

Of course, these Millesime claims are not credible if one knows about Pierre, the ghostwriter. But that's just it: till now, no one has.

And so while Pierre got full credit for Green Irish Tweed's evolutionary successor – the ultimate expression of his aquatic dreams, Cool Water – the lack of such a final product in the case of this salty-melon DNA meant Bourdon has never been considered a practitioner of this type of summer-salty perfumery, let alone its forefather (and salty fragrances happened to become extremely trendy again in the 2010s – see Calvin Klein Reveal for Men or Tom Ford Oud Minerale).

Here was a case where Pierre did not hold out – did not insist the world experience the ultimate realization of his idea. He just handed off Millesime to a huckster who claimed it'd been commissioned by a dead Arabian king.

Pierre's great '80s project had sapped him of the necessary resolve. He was now too weak to pursue the purest version of his concepts, too tired to accept more than one rejection before tossing the formula to Olivier for a small sum.

As a result, the house of Creed was about to receive for a pittance some of the most brilliant perfumes ever made.

Olivier Creed, attired in the dark button-down sported by George Raft in mob films and Regis Philbin on "Who Wants to be a Millionaire?" hunches over bottles bearing his surname, Dec. 7, 2000 (courtesy of Fred R. Conrad/The New York Times/Redux).

Chapter 8: The Castles

As the 1900s began to ebb in the public mind, a new millennium coming into view, the perfume world of Pierre Bourdon began to unravel, although he could have been forgiven for thinking temporarily just the opposite– that his fragmented life was finally coming together, coalescing.

His wife Francoise, who had refused to divorce Pierre for a decade, found in Roure perfumer Antoine Caron a new lover and finally ended the marriage – enabling Pierre to wed longtime partner Kathy.

Pierre also managed to double his salary at Takasago, in part via commissions on the sales of perfumes he'd devised (the amount taken in on Cool Water orders alone was ample).

"I had become the king of gold," he recalls to me.

Soon, though, his Midas touch seemed lost.

Takasago parted with the man who'd recruited Pierre to the company – John Roberts, who'd first made an impression on Pierre when they were the finalists in the contest to create Kouros. Roberts had lost that clash but had never held it against Pierre – in fact, he'd done just the opposite, humbly inviting his vanquisher to join forces with him.

That Pierre had agreed and then settled into Takasago (for what he presumed would be a very long haul) spoke to Roberts' humility and open-mindedness – and also Roberts' willingness to delegate responsibility, to trust those he considered exceptionally skilled. Roberts was technically Pierre's direct overseer, yet Roberts worked out of Takasago's American office and let Pierre run the French branch as Pierre saw fit. That Paris building was Pierre's castle, and deservedly so.

By contrast, Roberts' successor, Tony Griffiths, formerly of IFF, proved to be insecure and officious and inclined to elevate salespeople over scent-makers, in Pierre's recollection. His first move was to tell Pierre that the latter's salary was too high and would be cut and that Griffiths would also involve himself in the affairs of the Paris office, no matter that Pierre had run it smoothly and without issue for years. Griffiths then appointed another boss over Pierre – a salesman named Marc Rösti.

"I was berserk," Pierre recalls. "I was the one boiling the pot and this is how I was treated!"

So Pierre made the boldest possible demand to his Japanese superiors: Crown me the CEO of the French division – essentially the head of Takasago in all of Europe – or I'm out. The Japanese declined. Pierre, never one to ignore a vow, resigned.

Then he realized what he'd just done.

At that moment, his rage subsided, feeling betrayed by his own adrenaline, Pierre was left only with the fear and anxiety attendant to being unemployed. He now needed to find a perfumery concern that would hire him pronto, he thought. He couldn't be too picky about the ethos or politics of the place. Far worse than finding himself trapped again in a problematic corporate structure would be finding himself on the public dole.

Ah, humans, how we fabricate for ourselves the very issues that make us frantic.

This is how Pierre wound up creative director of Quest, a perfumery concern happy to hire him but owned by Unilever and beset by major issues related precisely to problematic corporate structuring:

As a cousin of Calvin Klein – Unilever had bought the clothier in 1989 – Quest was seen as unfairly positioned to win CK briefs and therefore blacklisted by other fashion designers with scent projects. No one wanted to compete against a firm with an undeserved leg-up. Or perhaps stated more precisely: What designer would invite in craftsmen essentially allied to another designer? Fashion is catty, not collaborative (or at least, that was the dynamic 30 years ago).

The second problem bedeviling Quest was also related to ownership: Unilever sold a tremendous amount of fragrance (it's the company behind Axe body spray, for example, which is created by the very same perfumers behind the scents sold at Saks, say), but Quest was not even on the Unilever core list. Somehow, its own corporate parent refused to hand Quest briefs – to let it compete for authorship.

"Quest suffered from a lack of credibility," Pierre recalls. Regretful he'd taken on such a bizarre and challenging task – the man was a perfumer, not a consultant expert in restructuring – Pierre nevertheless set out "to unblock" all these impediments to Quest's work.

* * *

Change was afoot in other domains, too – including the once-grand castle of Roure, Pierre's first workplace, the perfumery he perhaps should never have left, although the love triangle that saw him stay by his mistress' side had basically guaranteed that departure, no matter his feelings about the institution.

Pierre's old boss Jean Amic was soon to retire from his CEO role to pursue the study of the ancient pre-Roman civilization of the Etruscans, in Italy (and read all the serious tracts he hadn't had time for heretofore – including those of Jean Rostand, a noted French biologist-philosopher, and Claude Levi Strauss, an even more eminent intellectual, whom the New York Times dubbed the "father of modern anthropology" in his obituary headline).[45]

His successor, formerly the worldwide marketing director for Hoffman-La Roche's vitamin division, a Swiss man named Kuno Sommer, would soon be charged by the US Justice Department in 1999 for helping to fix the prices on vitamins A, B2, B5, C, E, and beta carotene during the 1990s as part of a cartel that included BASF and other vitamin firms.

Pleading guilty, Sommer would have to leave the CEO post within months of taking it from Amic, fined $100,000 and sentenced to four months in prison – becoming the first ever foreigner incarcerated in the US on a price-fixing charge.

Sommer served his time in a facility in West Virginia, where nobody from Givaudan (the new name for the Roure perfumery operation, after a merger of the two entities) came to visit save for Sommer's widely-beloved deputy, president Geoff Webster, a big, brash human who'd served as a pilot in the Vietnam War and garnered innumerable medals for valor in truly Rambo-esque circumstance.

Webster, who'd joined Roure in 1972, would rather shockingly retire in 2000 and even more shockingly receive a diagnosis thereafter of stage 4 brain cancer, from which he'd pass away at the age of 68.

Such is what became of Amic and the men who were supposed to succeed him – one erased by the world for running afoul of its orders ridiculously and one eliminated by its most savagely random ailment.

As for the castle of Creed, it continued to thrive on the strength of Pierre's perfumes, but a bizarre phenomenon, unjust to Olivier, though perhaps still more to Pierre, was beginning to take shape:

The faker was himself becoming the victim of forgery.

Observers of Creed's success, utterly unaware who was responsible for it but uncaring about attribution anyway, began to imitate the brand's scents. And we're not talking third-world counterfeiters either, a reality underlined by the fate of Millesime Imperial, Pierre's salty melon perfume, which Creed released in 1995 and later claimed had been made for a long-dead Saudi king.

The story begins with Sean Combs – aka P. Diddy – who, unlike most celebrities Creed cites, actually did adopt a Creed product as a signature scent – Millesime Imperial. It's unclear exactly what year he discovered the juice, but perhaps it was 1999, when he was dating Jennifer Lopez and Millesime Imperial was gaining something of a reputation among the wealthy.

Only a few years later, Diddy decided to launch a fragrance for his Sean John brand in tandem with Estee Lauder, which partnership chose Givaudan to formulate the juice. This team in place, someone in the mix then decided the scent would be a mass market copy of what Diddy already wore: Creed's Millesime Imperial.

A team of four perfumers at Givaudan took on the task of translating a brilliant but pricy formula into one that could be sold for mass market prices.

This dupe, dubbed Sean John Unforgivable, was released in 2006 – a time when Pierre Bourdon was already strongly considering retirement, utterly confused by the industry's bizarre semi-embrace of his life's work, tired of presenting himself via proxy, feeling essentially spurned by a subculture to which he had given everything. (Aren't all Cyrano de Bergeracs condemned to feel thusly at a certain point?)

In the first year Unforgivable was on the market, it made $150 million globally – none of which went to Pierre but none of which went to Olivier Creed either. For the first time, they were in the same spot – jointly ripped-off, the financial implications almost impossible to apprehend.

Unforgivable made so much money that one of the four creators at Givaudan – David Apel, who's now an exec at Symrise – told me his team inquired as to whether Unforgivable was the best-selling men's celebrity fragrance of all time (it's definitely close if not the outright winner, statistics on this area of the market being hard to come by).

Suddenly, it wasn't just Pierre whose ideas were being taken from him – because Olivier Creed, according to one perfumer who knows him well, actually had become convinced over the years that the scents he purchased off legit perfumers (after Pierre, there were others, as we'll see) had been the works of his own hand, the products of his own imagination (yes, this sounds psychotic; no, it's not an exaggeration).

"He embodied his double game so much that he ended up believing it in a funny way," this perfumer told me. "Sometimes, if I hadn't seen him for a week, he would hand me a paper blotter strip, wondering if I had smelled his latest idea. I brought it up to my nose, and looking bewildered and amused, I was like, 'But are you kidding me? This is what I gave you last week!'

"He sincerely believed he had created the idea."

The plundering of a Pierre perfume was now the co-opting of an Olivier idea, too, even if only due to the latter's severe delusion. Worse for Creed, the man imitating his material was employing the same language Olivier did in lying about work devised by others:

Diddy, in a 2007 interview with Women's Wear Daily, on the scent's success – the italics my own:

"This is something that only I could do, because it is me. And if I'm authentic, I gotta be myself. I can't all of a sudden have the number-one fragrance and start being like Armani or Ralph, start trying to fit in. If anything, I'm trying to stand out even more."

Still, this new phenomenon didn't diminish Creed's wealth, though it failed to increase it; and as Olivier continued pursuing Pierre's rejections, living parasitically off the real perfumer's painstaking efforts, one can't say he was at all chastened by the experience, let alone reformed.

To this day, the Givaudan team of four has no idea it was actually cloning a Bourdon scent – if any of them is reading this, he or she is finding out right now. An astounding episode, as I see it – though Pierre himself had neither time nor inclination in the 1990s to marvel at such stories. The man was accustomed to being aped, however unfairly, and was preoccupied anyway with turning around the business of his new employer, Unilever's Quest perfumery.

Say what you will about Pierre Bourdon, and certainly some of his former colleagues consider him arrogant and aloof while those who know him better might call him exceedingly fragile, but the man never stopped pushing ahead in the industry, even once he was so afraid of rejection he was resignedly handing Olivier formulas he'd have done better to keep developing on his own, under his own byline.

So Pierre went about legitimizing Quest as a company, the achievement of which task depended in part on the friends he'd made in the industry already, who didn't fail to come through. Michael Foerster of Lancaster, the company that had launched Cool Water and Joop! Homme, briefed Pierre on a new Joop! scent that would be named Nightflight and then selected his entry as the winner. The folks at Yves Saint Laurent entrusted Pierre with the creation of a new, slightly lighter version of Kouros. Victories followed at Ted Lapidus and Rochas.

Pierre could never have won these contests had he not been briefed, and that's precisely why he was so grateful to the friends who allowed him to compete. In this sense, then, his reshaping of Quest was an implicit rebuke of his twisted, Stockholm Syndrome-y relationship with Olivier Creed, whose monopoly on Pierre's once-rejected work meant such scents were never shown to 99 percent of industry deciders and therefore could never be considered for wins.

That said, there was one triumph at Quest whose creation Pierre had no hand in – a scent authored by the most unlikely of figures. Incorporating the flavoring ingredient ethyl maltol and built atop a patchouli base, the creation not only won its brief but inaugurated an entirely new genre of perfume: the gourmands, or those scents appealing for a smell seemingly edible (which tend these days to evoke chocolate, vanilla, coffee or, believe it or not, cotton candy).

This triumphant brief was for Thierry Mugler Angel, a 1992 release, and the surprise nose behind it was Olivier Cresp, the brother of Francoise Cresp, or the woman who refused to divorce Pierre for a full decade after he left her for a younger mate.

Yes, Pierre's partner in making Quest a legitimate player in the industry was none other than his ex-brother-in-law. How the French manage such dynamics I don't understand, yet that they do is undeniable.

(Although to be fair, bizarre beauty industry trysts bloom in the US, too; Estee Lauder had an affair with the head of IFF's forerunner company and a future IFF chairman – Arnold Lewis van Ameringen – before reconciling with her husband and then asking Ameringen anyway to create her company's first perfumed products.)

Also undeniable: the project to propel Quest into the big-time was a success – so much so that in November 2006, Givaudan (aka Roure, aka the temple of perfumery at which Pierre began his career) announced the acquisition of Quest for $2.3 billion.

Of course, by that point, Pierre had already been gone from the company for a full decade. He had never needed the validation of such an offer to convince him of his success in making Quest relevant. He was well aware of what he'd done – so much so that he asked for a raise in salary in 1995, despite his superiors' claims that he already was paid as much as the president of Unilever.

When his request was denied, he left Quest – just walked out the door – but not out of a fit of pique or in arrogant outburst. In fact, the request of the raise was something of a red herring. Pierre had already decided to leave for reasons involving the very core of his being – he only would have stayed had Unilever lavished him with mindboggling money – asking for it was simply a shot worth taking.

But why leave a good thing anyway? Pierre had left Roure because his affair had necessitated it, and Takasago because his boss had been replaced by an exec he considered a boob. But he'd built Quest into a perfumery power – into the sort of contender, if not champ, Marlon Brando had spoken so movingly about wanting to be. Why wouldn't he remain in place and now fight for the title – against power punchers Givaudan and Firmenich and IFF?

The answer involves a meeting Pierre had while still at Quest, near the end of his tenure:

He had been summoned to the office of Maurice Roger, longtime president of Parfums Dior, the operation once managed by Pierre's father, whom Pierre never could impress. Pierre had long believed that creating a Dior scent would make him feel whole (of course, such an achievement could never make up for unreceived paternal love, but never mind that for now).

Roger had a project he wanted Pierre to helm – but before he would discuss it, he asked to learn more about Quest, a firm with which he was still unfamiliar. And so a Quest salesperson at the meeting gave a brief presentation on the outfit.

"When he learned of our Unilever affiliation," Pierre recalls, "his blood swirled, and with the abruptness to which he was accustomed, he attacked us."

"The interview is over!" Roger shouted at Pierre. "It is out of the question for me to brief the owner of Calvin Klein! Please leave my office!"

Roger stood up and literally pushed both the salesperson and Pierre out of the office. But that order mattered – the salesperson having been ejected slightly ahead of Pierre, he started for the elevator while Pierre was still standing in the office doorway. That's when Roger tapped Pierre on the shoulder and whispered into his ear:

"There is a rumor going around the perfume world that you want to change creameries (this is a French expression used for a person who takes his business elsewhere). If so, when you do, let me know – because I will have two projects that I would like you to work on."

And so it was *that* promise – the chance to work on a Dior fragrance finally – perhaps two! – that led Pierre to demand a ridiculously massive raise at Quest and then leave the Unilever firm altogether. It was never about money or prestige. He was never a prima donna wide receiver, an uber-talented but insufferably egotistical star (mostly).

It was just that Roger's offer of two Dior developments represented Pierre's final chance to create a scent there. Roger was known to be nearing retirement, beset by chronic polyarthritis, or debilitating inflammation of more than five joints across the body. Nobody in the industry knew what would become of Parfums Dior after Roger's departure – except that Bernard Arnault, billionaire chairman of Dior's parent company, LVMH, was likely to involve himself in the transition despite knowing relatively little about perfume.

Here was an opportunity Pierre couldn't squander – one whose window could expire at any moment.

The ghost perfumer went for it.

Chapter 9: Ambition

Having successfully turned around both Takasago and Quest, Pierre was hotly pursued upon becoming a free agent: He received eight job offers – or one for each rejection of Cool Water, a parallel that perhaps meant more to him than industry colleagues realized.

In truth, Pierre had never let himself forget or forgive that series of refusals, treating it instead as a chip on his shoulder, an insult to be rendered ridiculous by an incredibly fecund, brilliant career. Indeed, the eight Cool Water passes were to him was what the six-round wait to be drafted was for Tom Brady – *a challenge*.

All the same, Pierre didn't let that history affect his decision-making now. The best offer had been made by Firmenich, a Swiss flavors and fragrances concern that was becoming a major rival of Givaudan (aka Roure, Pierre's first employer).

Or, rather, the offer came not from Firmenich the company but Patrick Firmenich the man. A scion of the private company's founders, he was then, in 1995, in charge of international fine fragrance strategy but would become the company's CEO in 2002 and its board chairman in 2016.

His offer to Pierre was simple: the man running Firmenich's Paris office (which was technically located just outside the city, in Neuilly) was retiring – why not come on board as his successor?

Pierre would then be in charge of perhaps the greatest collection of perfumery talents in the world – the boss of luminaries such as Alberto Morillas, Jacques Cavallier, Annick Menardo and Annie Buzantian – the four of whom were about to change the fragrance market forever with the 1996 release of Armani Acqua di Gio pour Homme (it was projected to do a respectable $30 million in sales in its first year but wound up instead becoming the best-selling masculine in the world for 15 years).

But Pierre Bourdon remained devoted as ever to the lover who had become his second wife. And so just as he declined a return to Roure when Jean Amic refused to bring Kathy back to the Paris office, so, too, did Pierre decline Patrick Firmenich's overture when the latter balked at employing her.

Yes, Pierre had abandoned his first wife – but his romantic devotion to her successor was proving, with each job he declined, ever more remarkable. Or perhaps Pierre was natively inclined to take chances, to revel in outsider opportunities, to play the role of winsome underdog, an honest cop in a corrupt city.

But whatever the reason, Pierre decided to accept the riskiest of the proposals made to him during this period. A perfume industry veteran named Horst Gerberding had bought three perfume companies – firms in America, Germany and France. He was now uniting them under the banner of the US company's name – Fragrance Resources – and wanted Pierre, as president of the French division, to set up and run a Paris office for the company as well as reorganize the production facility Gerberding had bought in the South of France, in Grasse.

"Once again, I found myself in a bad way, [in a job] that could ruin my career if I failed," Pierre recalls of his decision. "But, on the strength of my two previous experiences, I felt surer of myself. The offsets for the risk involved were a salary equal to Takasago's, sales commissions, stock options and the ability to hire Kathy."

Quickly, Pierre found office space at 226 Boulevard Saint-Germain, a five-minute walk from his home that therefore wouldn't saddle him with a long commute. With no less alacrity did he have the laboratory constructed inside the new digs.

"My haste was explained by the fact that I knew that Maurice Roger, the president of Dior, had two briefs for me," Pierre says.

Indeed, his change of employer and office were minor developments, in his thinking, in comparison with the chance to make a Dior scent, which had been a lifelong goal, if an unhealthy one. In fact, one can see Pierre's willingness to let Olivier Creed take credit for all his work in the same manner: the scents hadn't been destined for Dior, so what did it matter what became of them or to whom they were credited?

Finally free of Quest, Pierre was able to visit Roger and ask for the Dior assignments he had been promised. There was a finality about the proceedings. Roger was not just in ill-health physically, but emotionally; the advent of consumer testing in Europe in the 1990s meant a man who'd spent decades collaborating with perfumers, assured of his artistic judgment, was no longer allowed to trust such intimacy and intuition.

For years, Roger had mocked the focus groups whose results dictated the direction of scents at other institutions. His loudly professed motto was "Fewer tests and more testicles!" Obviously, a world ever more driven by data and consumed by political correctness could no longer abide such an executive.

But for now Roger still ruled, in the twilight of a storied career but with the same sense of adventure, the same boldness, for which he had become known decades earlier. One day not long after Pierre had set up the Fragrance Resources office, Roger burst in uninvited. Pierre had wanted to get his office fully up-and-running before contacting Roger, but the latter was neither patient nor hesitant. If he wanted to get something, he went after it.

And so in an unfinished office of an essentially new company, Roger sat down before Pierre and began to speak. "They say that you are not too delicate, so I bring you a brief, which will be a kind of trial run, will allow me to judge what is in your belly. If you disappoint me, we'll leave it there. Otherwise, it will be followed by a much larger one."

Roger then outlined to Pierre his plan for a new fresh feminine fragrance that would eventually be titled Eau Svelte, concluding:

"Enough verbal diarrhea! *Salut!* I await your news."

Roger then left. The interview had lasted barely 10 minutes. Dumbfounded by the behavior and departure, Pierre said not a word. But that stupefaction didn't last long – here was the chance of a lifetime for Pierre to make just the perfume his father had always lauded, for a brand that had always eluded him. He had but a few weeks to get it done.

"I took to the stove," Pierre recalls. A month after submitting his entry, Roger called him. "Well you've lost, but your scent came in second," said the Dior boss. "As I am satisfied with your work and to console you, I invite you to work on a new feminine. Make me a sweet and caressing fragrance."

Roger hung up before Pierre could even open his mouth. Months later, once Roger and Pierre had become friends, the former actually admitted to the latter that he had indeed won the Eau Svelte contest. Roger had just thought it unwise to reward the new kid on the block so soon, and so deferred Pierre's rise, overlooked his win, to keep him humble.

What Roger didn't know was that Pierre was already far humbler than his brusqueness might indicate. In fact, Pierre meekly turned over his runner-up Eau Svelte juice – a fruity-floral scent – to Olivier Creed, who dubbed it Spring Flower, claiming it had been created in 1951 for Audrey Hepburn.[46]

Bourdon was thereby denied credit for inventing the fruity-floral feminine scent that has inspired a million other juices put on the market since. But Pierre no longer had the stomach to consider what might have been, to hold fast to his ideas regardless of their first reception.

Pierre faced forward exclusively – and he had a new Dior assignment anyway. *Make me a sweet and caressing fragrance,* Roger had requested for Dior. So Pierre spent three months preparing samples for his meetings with Marie-Christine Wittgenstein, the Dior marketer in charge of the project, none of which she liked.

"I was beginning to despair and regret choosing Fragrance Resources," he recalls, believing his work wasn't being received well because of his relatively small coterie of salespeople and evaluators and supporters.

But this Dior marketer did keep mentioning Feminite du Bois, the 1992 women's scent Pierre co-created (with Christopher Sheldrake) three years earlier for Shiseido, legendary for being the first cedar-dominant scent for women. For being woodsy and womanly simultaneously. And so Pierre began to realize that what the Dior overseer wanted was not something entirely new but a riff on a brilliant mix Pierre had already made.

For so many perfumers, this would have been a welcome epiphany – tweaking a formula slightly for the big bucks of LVMH, Dior's parent, would be easy work, a no-brainer, win-win move. But not for Bourdon, whose integrity kept him from ever using the same formula twice. He takes pains to argue that he pushed Cool Water far enough away from Green Irish Tweed for the two to be considered sufficiently different.[47]

"I had to move away as far as possible from the original and produce a work on the same theme, but orchestrated in a completely different way," Pierre recalls of his Dior mission once he understood it. Perhaps he was disappointed by the derivative nature of the task, but at least,

Pierre knew how to pull it off:

He grafted onto the Feminite formula a module from Lancome Tresor and borrowed elements from Guerlain Shalimar to obtain the "soft and caressing" aspect Dior desired. Wittgenstein, the marketer, appreciated it and forwarded it to Maurice Roger, whose reaction would determine not just whether Pierre had succeeded in this instance but whether he'd ever author a Dior scent at all – his desperate dream since he was a young man. There was a sense that even if Roger survived his health scares, no matter how long he stayed, his replacement would surely be found lacking.

Suggestive of just that: Maurice Roger later proposed in the late-'90s to Pierre that the perfumer "olfactively illustrate" a western or buccaneer film by using notes of rum, leather, and gunpowder. Intrigued, Pierre had a hunter friend bring him fired rifle cartridges so he could study their aroma.

Roger was enthusiastic about the juice concocted as a result of this study, but, having departed Dior in early 1996, he no longer had the power to turn a Pierre Bourdon perfume into an actual product. Pierre still rues this – that he couldn't get to market what he and Roger knew was a fascinating work – what could have been Dior's '90s masculine (he did sell a version of this to the license holder for Smith & Wesson guns, but the idea was shoddily and cheaply executed).

Of course, those who'd taken over for Roger didn't seem to appreciate or comprehend the idea.

So this women's fragrance slightly based on Feminite du Bois was indeed Pierre's last chance to make a scent for the company his father had helmed, for the institution whose approval he'd sought for decades.

And then one day, Pierre got a call – it was from Roger: ""I'll be right there," Roger said. "I am coming to spend two weeks with you. My team is instructed not to disturb me. As for you, cancel all your appointments. We will finalize your PLB 255."

That last alphanumeric code was the internal name at Dior for this new fragrance, which Roger and Pierre did spend the next few days polishing, finishing. When the marathon session ended, Roger said, "You've got a 99 percent chance of winning. I must present your perfume to my board of directors, [but they] will, as usual, endorse my choice. "

Pierre was at a meeting of Fragrance Resources presidents in La Tour-de-Peilz, Switzerland, a hamlet situated between Montreux and Vevey on Lake Geneva, when he received the call from Roger that he'd attained the final 1 percent – that is, the board had approved his feminine creation, which would ultimately take the name "Dolce Vita."

It was a rapturous moment.

"Suddenly, I informed Horst, present at this meeting of which I became the hero," Pierre says. "With a Dior, a small company like ours now belonged to the big leagues!"

When Dolce Vita launched in June of 1995, Pierre spent the day hanging about the Museum of Fairground Arts in Paris' 12th Arrondissement – a venue open since 1996 featuring old midway rides and arcade games. Pierre has never explained to me why he chose to celebrate there, but he hasn't had to – the man had felt destined since childhood to create a Dior perfume. Now having done it, he'd made good on his childhood promise – had retroactively justified his obsession. Why not patronize a place dedicated to what we excitedly once dreamed?

"I was on a cloud," Pierre recalls.

That night, he went out drinking with Roger and a journalist, imbibing entire bottles of champagne. Gleefully blotto, he kept turning over the same amazing idea in his head: "I who had lived my childhood and my adolescence entranced by the legend of Dior Perfumes, I had just participated in the writing of a short story of its pages, me, the son of one of its founders!"

From left to right, Pierre at the launch of Dolce Vita, with Parfums Dior President Maurice Roger and perfume bottle designer Serge Mansau

Of course, whether the creation of a scent could compensate for years of unrequited filial tenderness was a major question, albeit one better left for another day (perhaps even as soon as the following morning, in the midst of an almost philosophically torturous hangover, one of those post-party moments of reckoning in which everything taken for granted just hours earlier seems suddenly in question).

The more apt inquiry on that joyous, bubbly-soaked night was perhaps not what remained for Pierre to achieve – he was doing the work he loved, after all, even if he was so brainwashed as to require no real payment for it in within one effed relationship and even if his Dior release marked a career climax – but what remained for the fraud who effed him over, much of whose life was a lie, most of its climaxes unearned (and perhaps unfulfilling for that reason):

Olivier Creed.

What was this man still looking to gain?

Olivier was a known habitue of the art auctions at the Hotel Drouot in Paris, which is to say, he seemed as flush with cash as ever.

He had indeed divorced his wife Fabienne, in whose name the Creed perfume boutique – just off the Champs Elysees, a kilometer from the Arc de Triomphe – was now registered, perhaps as part of a settlement – but Olivier nevertheless planned to open boutiques in London, Milan, Los Angeles, Tokyo, Singapore, Berlin and Moscow.[48] Again, if his circumstances were reduced, or by divorce halved, Olivier never showed it.

The man had the companionship of a girlfriend. And, bizarrely, the approbation and kinship of many actual perfumers, whom he'd also managed to con into believing his creation myths. What more could be added to that, and why bother? How exciting could IP-sponging and epiphany-story fabrication continue to be?

These are unanswerable questions – not least because I wouldn't trust Olivier's knowledge of his own self. We do things long before we understand why – if we ever shall at all. And that goes for the less complicated among us, let alone the deluded and entitled ones.

But a review of the record – Creed's release of a summery watermelon scent from Pierre as Millesime Imperial in 1995, his release of Pierre's rejected Issey Miyake bid as Silver Mountain Water about the same time – leaves one with this impression:

Having received a bit of attention in a small subculture, Olivier couldn't help but lust after considerably more. He'd had a taste. Now, he had a craving. Olivier Creed: In the 1980s and 1990s, a charlatan; at the turn of the Millennium, a man desperately chasing the dragon.

Hell, in the hyping of Silver Mountain Water, Olivier claimed he'd skied on the French national team (if he did, I've yet to see the proof, not that I'm).[49]

And if Olivier Creed really did want to go bigger than ever – if he desired to become known to the wider world as a master perfumer – he was almost implausibly in luck, his timing uncanny: As the mid-'90s gave way to that pre-Y2K period that seems somehow so innocent in retrospect, if only for immediately preceding September 11th, a new tool was emerging that could take even the most minor of expert figures or celebrities and render them globally known, everywhere recognized.

It was called the Internet, and though its greatest possibilities – to increase commerce, to spread celebrity, to distort the truth – were yet unknown, let alone explored, it nevertheless already had the power to amplify a liar's version of events – and to efface the person actually responsible for their being set in motion.

The tale of the con-man and the cologne-creator was about to go cyber.

Chapter 10: The Hustler

I t was the end of the Disco '70s. Dale Dewey was a sandy-haired, high school ski-bum in Michigan who raced downhill and taught others to do the same.

As he approached his senior year, having never left home for scholastic adventure, unlike his brother, who'd attended a prep school in Massachusetts, Dale decided to go abroad, to France of all places, and close out his studies there – a decision his later pursuits retroactively justified but must've struck his peers as exceptionally odd at the time.

One imagines his collegiate crew reacting similarly just a couple years later, when he spent four collegiate semesters studying not on the Vermont campus of Middlebury, where he skied on the B team, training alongside the six-member varsity squad, but on the Parisian grounds of Sciences Po, the distinguished alma mater of Pierre Bourdon.

Not that Dale Dewey, Midwesterner with flaxen hair and a bulbous nose, yet knew who Pierre was or the facts of his timing: that concurrent to Dale's sojourn in the City of Light, Pierre and his wife Francoise were finally joining the paid, elite ranks of Roure perfumers in that same place, having toiled a half-decade in the company's school in the south of France.

Also unknown to Dale in Paris: An aristocratic tailor named Olivier

Creed – who, having failed for a few years to generate an interesting scent, was on a predatory hunt for a far more captivating composer.

By the end of the century, neither man would still be a mystery to him. In fact, Dale would be so intimately caught up in the work of each, he'd have very definite opinions about both and no compunction about sharing them.

"There are many people who believe that Pierre Bourdon might be the greatest perfumer of all time," he told me 10 minutes into our conversation about his crazy career and its intersection with our foremost players. Ten minutes after that: "It was clear that Olivier Creed did nothing."

But Dale Dewey did not immediately enter the fragrance world after his university days – that would come later and involve ultimately the greatest technological revolution since the days of Gutenberg.

Dale Dewey's first claim to fame, if it can be called that, emanated from a mid-century modernist office at 300 Park Avenue – a fine structure from 1955 greatly overshadowed by its ornate and lavish counterpart across the street: 301 Park – otherwise known as the Waldorf-Astoria.

Then again, what better metaphor than this neighborly contrast for educated and itinerant Dale – who'd get his kicks not from personal primping or treatments but from their commercial sale?

See, 300 Park was no fancy hotel – it was the 26-story corporate headquarters of the Colgate-Palmolive company – that all-American maker of zingy toothpaste and phosphorescent dishwashing soap.

Dale joined Colgate in 1984 and, as a brand manager for five years, helped launch Lournay, one of the first skincare lines marketed to those with very sensitive outer layers, emerging a more experienced seller – a hybrid of Loman and Barnum — with an intact Francophile soul.

Hence his ensuing gigs: Dewey spent three years managing accounts at fragrance multinational Firmenich and another four years doing the same at rival Givaudan. These jobs took him to years-long residences in Geneva, London and Paris. Having already spent a half-decade in New York, Dewey, though unknown to perfumers and consumers alike, was perhaps one of the world's foremost experts on the commerce of scents.

His long education in the fragrance game complete, he began in the mid-'90s to try and revolutionize the same. He'd seen how little data was involved in certain major perfumery decisions – sometimes none – Chanel lost $50 million by deciding to re-launch its Bois Noir fragrance as Egoiste, for instance, without having studied the matter prior – so Dale launched a fragrance market research firm, which was hired by, among others, Chanel, Procter & Gamble and Lancome. Dale sold the company in two years to product-tracker *par excellence* NPD.

Dale also had the idea of building out a fragrance retailer on a main drag in tony Greenwich, Connecticut, of the belief he could be the next vendor of Giorgio, that an equivalent to Rodeo Drive would surely arise in the area given the sudden density of hedge funds there situated. This didn't work out, though the man was hardly deterred – hell, he just decided to kiss bricks and mortar goodbye.

In the fall of 1998, he jumped into the Internet – deciding to create a web site that retailed fine fragrance, no matter that the web couldn't transmit a whiff to potential customers seated at home (it still can't, though scientists are actively working on this challenge in 2021 and it's conceivable that you could have various samples compounded inside your own home at your leisure with a certain kit – the challenge is different from that of 3D printing but perhaps by degree instead of kind).

Dewey was also not the first entrepreneur to propose such a site — Fragrancecounter.com and Perfumania.com already existed. But these two sites acquired brand-name scents through grey-market vendors, rendering their wares, especially on the high end, of unverifiable authenticity. Moreover, Dewey already understood the Lycos-AltaVista-Yahoo-Google nature of Internet pioneering:

You don't have to be the first site devoted to a task – say, searching the web – to become, essentially, its first. Make your venture indispensable, preeminent, and the public, its memory shortened by the churn of tech turnover, will confer upon it far more than just legitimacy. It will hand over its sense of time.

So Dale had a chance to build the Internet's first true perfume vendor, one whose wares would be acquired entirely through brand-authorized channels. He raised $5 million and hired as his marketing officer a graduate of Georgetown's School of Foreign Service with an executive MBA from NYU.

He named the site jasmin.com and began talking it up in the press months ahead of its launch. Already fragrance sales in department stores had begun to plateau – sales in the year before the site's launch, 1998, were $2.9 billion, up just 1% from 1997. Dale was going to shake things up, do things differently (he was also wise enough to realize how slim a percentage of such department store sales he needed to put the site in the black; a small pilfering from Macy's would constitute a major payoff for him).

Dale also worked his contacts unstintingly. He set up meetings with both the venture capital investors in beauty products-retailer Ulta and Procter & Gamble, which hadn't yet shed its prestige fragrance division. Both sides told him they wouldn't invest in his internet adventure unless the other did, so he wound up telling each, as Bob Geldof did with Live-Aid bands, that the other was in before it actually was and thus secured two commitments (technically, he says he merely claimed to each side that the other had yet to decline).

In fact, Ulta itself wound up handling the fulfillment of orders placed on Jasmin.com, via its SAP-logistics warehouse.

On Procter: Dale realized the only way to drag folks to a new web outpost at that time was to carry something unattainable elsewhere – a fragrance exclusively sold on the site. Procter agreed to do just that with a masculine from Hugo Boss, Boss Bottled, so long as the site launched by a certain date and autumn fashion season wasn't missed (actually, Jasmin wound up going online at 2 am the day after the deadline, but nobody on the P&G side noticed this two-hour tardiness, and Dale never brought it up – the penalty for it would have been $2.5 million).

More on Procter: It wasn't just Dale's words that won him the deal but figures he had independently calculated on the profit and loss P&G experienced when launching a fragrance via a traditional department store-reliant scheme. Dale knew the million ways department stores knocked percentages off what it paid Procter – his market research days benefiting him greatly. He then displayed by contrast – via PowerPoint, #1999, #theArtistFormerlyKnownasClippy – what P&G would see in return for an internet launch.

That the department store was already dead was a suggestion neither provocative nor inspired. Dale and the corporate-types he pitched by now agreed on this – if it took the rest of America a couple decades further to decide finally once and for all the same – to write the obituary – that was their own mistake, a delay or distortion in public opinion due to nostalgia or fear, to tendencies and passions Luddite and maybe slightly lyrical.

But that Dale had the answer? This P&G agreed on based on his PowerPoint figures alone. "Who gave you our numbers?" execs asked him of his profit and loss figures on fragrance launches.

"I just know," Dale replied. "I've been in business a long time."

It was this confidence, or rather, the accuracy that underpinned it, that not only convinced Procter to buy into an exclusive Hugo Boss fragrance launch on Jasmin but to invest $12 million in a joint marketing campaign.

But Dale was not done. He found a New York company called Arcade Marketing innovating in the world of fragrance test-strip ads – you know the tech – those children's storybook-style flaps under which a facsimile of a scent has been pasted.

Arcade had created a frosted plastic pouch that could be attached to a magazine ad. Opening it didn't merely give you access to an odorant smear – it gave you a splash sample of the perfume you could wear. It looks like a slim Tide Pod (I can say from a vantage point two decades later).

So Dewey came up with a two-pronged plan: Mail out samples speedily to potential customers who request them – he believes his company sent out 40 million samples during its short life, via mail and magazines – and convey the juice in magazines with a fillip of NC-17 coquetry (a more liberated European aesthetic, say).

The double-sided ad that resulted featured a wearable offering of Boss Bottled on one side while the other boasted a visibly topless, dark-nippled La Scala ballerina holding above her head – like some sort of profane *tallis* – a wavy, silken, diaphanous sheet, meant to represent the aura offered by perfume.

JASMIN.COM
EXPERIENCE THE WORLD OF FRAGRANCES

Introducing BOSS Hugo Boss. Exclusively at JASMIN.COM

That Dewey managed to convince ad folks at Hearst and Conde Nast and Time to run this erotic and unfiltered photo is amazing. It appeared in Vogue, Cosmo, Harper's Bazaar, Esquire.[50] But they weren't alone: Dewey ultimately convinced the ad departments of *22 of the 24 magazines* he petitioned to run it (Men's Health was one of the nays; its ownership by Rodale, a starchy family-owned publisher in the middle of Pennsylvania, meant it didn't quite share other rags' more liberal/accommodating commercial ethos).

Dale also paid for Jasmin to sponsor a release event for the Kevin Costner flick "For the Love of the Game." He got baseball pitcher Al Leiter to hawk the site (he'd just won the World Series with the Marlins two years prior).

Dale Dewey, Laurice Rahme and Annette Green, president of the Fragrance Foundation, at the launch of Jasmin.com. (courtesy of Dale)

On a certain level, none of that matters now. Jasmin fell victim not long after its birth to the ensuing dotcom bubble burst. Dewey had projected that 10 percent of all fragrance sales might migrate online from stores. He thought, if I could only snag just half of those online sales, given my first mover advantage, I'll suddenly have 5 effing percent of all perfume sales in the States. Which would have worked.

Only he noticed just 0.5% of fragrance sales moving online despite his crazy ad spree and no big increase in sight.

"We were just so far ahead of the curve," he tells me now, without bitterness – sounding no less boyish or enthusiastic than he always does. "Just so far ahead of the curve."

To whit: Online perfume and cosmetic sales are estimated to hit $12.2 billion in 2021.[51]

But there's another side to the story of Jasmin – whose domain name today leads to a porn site — one uncompromised by the quick undoing of the original scheme – because Dale desired not just an exclusive scent to lure perfume enthusiasts but also an exclusive brand.

The brand he wound up signing? Creed, naturally. Jasmin had the sole right to sell Creed scent online in the US.

Which meant that the ski bum from Michigan turned internet impresario – the man who'd spent years studying at Bourdon's Parisian alma mater – was now somehow the gatekeeper of Pierre's work in the world's largest consumer market.

And on the flip side of the same coin, Dale was now equally responsible for covering up that creative process, for promulgating the lies that had taken Creed this far. Jasmin's Dec. 16, 1999, press release about the deal is nauseating even by the standards already-quoted in this book, claiming – among so many others – as Creed clients King George III, Oscar Wilde, Francis Bacon, Jackie Kennedy, Paul Newman, Princess Grace and Tom Cruise.

When Jasmin first went live, its site offered 63 brands. That number was later cut to 35. Some of the brands were represented by just a single release. And yet, from its launch until the unfortunate end a couple years later, Jasmin carried all the signature Creeds, including Green Irish Tweed, Millesime Imperial and Silver Mountain Water – all Pierre productions, of course. Not to mention Spring Flower, which the site called "the Scent of Royalty" when it was merely a rejected Dior submission by Pierre.

Because of Creed's primacy at Jasmin, the alternate history in which the site outlasts the web's lean years and ultimately becomes an internet success is mindbogglingly fascinating. It means the Amazon for scent – the go-to destination for expensive online fragrance buys – would have likely featured most prominently not Armani, Versace, YSL, Dior, Tom Ford or Chanel but Creed – Creeds created by Pierre Bourdon for no more payment than a suit each and the promise of a massive sum on the day of his retirement.

Pierre, his name nevertheless still hidden, would have had the satisfaction of knowing that the entire fragrance-buying world had to reckon online with his work before deciding, if it should, to purchase another perfumer's.

Or would that not be satisfaction for him – would the greater primacy of his perfume pose a greater vexation for a man denied all attribution by a smug member of the party circuit?

In truth, it's a fictive set-up. Because while Dale's Jasmin venture sunk, Amazon most certainly didn't. It's not only the most successful of the Web 1.0 survivors; it's the most far-reaching and powerful retailer the world has ever known.

And the work of Pierre Bourdon is splashed all across it – and more prominently than that, the work of one of his students is one of its bestsellers, its sales exponential, beyond prodigious.

How did Amazon get in the business of promoting Pierre and his pupil?

Well, one has to examine the ultimate decline in the relationship between Pierre and Olivier after the year 2000 – and the way Olivier's greediness for just one more Bourdon blockbuster accidentally bestowed power on a worldwide band of pirates based in Dubai, determined to clone Creed work without recompense.

CHAPTER 10: THE HUSTLER

Or, what happened when Olivier pushed too hard one too many times…and the scent-poachers swarmed.

Chapter 11: Youth

In autumn 2020, amidst a pandemic, 4 ounces of a Creed perfume produced nearly a decade earlier were put up for sale on eBay for $50,000 (plus $4.75 in shipping).

In a sense, this floated sale on the secondary market, this appreciation of a juice Creed first sold for hundreds, mirrored the one that saw the company change hands for the first time earlier that year – the billion-buck transaction that allowed Olivier Creed to cash out of a venture in which he was never, insofar as earnest thought, brainstorming, intellectual churn, is concerned, the principal investor – just the beneficiary – *always* the beneficiary.

Aventus was the end of Creed. Aventus was also the beginning. But above all, Aventus was the stretch, the greedy grab that expanded an imbalanced relationship between a genius and a fraud into a multigenerational epic.

* * *

The year was 1995. Pierre had finally created his one Dior scent – whose name the reader might perhaps read as ironic, Fellini-esque, an admission that life is so much more complicated – and bitter – than we can often bear to concede: "La Dolce Vita."

By this point, Pierre's father Rene had been retired from Parfums

Dior for 13 years. Still, Rene could have reacted to Pierre's success at the company Rene had overseen for so long and praised so highly. Could have welcomed Pierre into the club, so to speak – conceded finally his son had made the grade.

But earlier, Rene Bourdon, at the age of 70, had not only left Dior but Paris proper, had returned to the north of the country, married a second time, to a far younger woman, who'd borne him a child – moves Pierre neither condemned nor condoned. "I don't have to judge him," Pierre said to me somewhat enigmatically. "He did what he wanted with his life."

No, Rene did not compliment Pierre in 1995, from the hamlet to which the father had repaired once he was finished with city life, with aspirational living more generally. Striving.

Only a year later, in 1996, when Pierre turned 50, did Rene tell him for the *first* time he was proud of his son. And Rene repeated that line exactly once – seven years after that, in 2003, when Rene was on his deathbed, in Salpêtrière Hospital, whose name indicates its original usage as a gunpowder factory.

On May 8, 2003, at the age of 90, Rene Bourdon died.

"He was buried in the cemetery of Crennes, under the windows of his birthplace," Pierre says. "A lifetime of hard work and travel around the world to get right back to square one!"

That Rene felt tremendous affection toward his son Pierre does not doubt. That he didn't express it save for those two belated occasions was a wrong by nearly any standard of parentage. That such withholding nevertheless left an impression on Pierre, such that we might not know him without it, is a knotty, awful notion.

(Do we bless the fatherly tennis-tutelage-torture of Andre Agassi because we'd never have seen Sampras-Agassi otherwise? If not, how tolerant are we to be of lesser misbehavior– what about Rene's great pride in his son's work – obvious to a certain extent and yet never verbally expressed save for those tardy occasions? Pierre to me: "I think I was moved, not by ambition, but by the terror of being a failure.")

And yet life is more complex still. Because while Rene never said much to Pierre in the way of encouragement, he took it upon himself to do what Pierre himself could not: He actually wore the animalic, sex-panthery perfume Pierre created in 1981, Yves Saint-Laurent Kouros (a scent I wear myself but others regard as urinous).

"It was, perhaps, for him a roundabout way of paying me a compliment," Pierre muses.

But there was another death a couple years earlier, whose meaning was not a cause of retrospection and rumination but foreboding: Horst Gerberding, the German heir who'd united three companies under the Fragrance Resources banner and made Pierre its president, passed away at just 75 at the start of the Aughts.

Which move was followed by the board of the company dispatching Horst's salesman son to the office at 226 Boulevard Saint-Germain to ask Pierre for the perfumer's role as head of the French subsidiary. Suddenly a magical run was over – Pierre's success used almost as grounds for his dismissal.

Under the Fragrance Resources banner, Pierre had created The Good Life for Davidoff, a melony men's summer perfume still legendary in some parts and another notch in his long run of successes for that brand (a vintage bottle of 2.5 oz was priced in July 2021 at $350 on eBay).

Dr. Ernst Schneider, owner of Davidoff, embraces Pierre at the launch of
Good Life Women, 1999.

He'd opened an Italian office in Como and won Ferragamo and
Gianfranco Ferre briefs. In Spain he created perfumes for Myrugia
and Puig. In the US, for Coty and Procter & Gamble.

The 2007 fine fragrance sales of the company totaled 40 million
Euros.

And yet, that very same year, an industry trade magazine asked the
chairman of Fragrance Resources, the son of Horst, how such a small

company would fare against Givaudan and IFF and Symrise, these leviathans of scented liquid.

"We are (core)-listed at Procter & Gamble as at Coty," answered Friedrich Gerberding. "We know how to provide everything they need. In addition, even if the time has come for consolidation, this industry remains a profession where people come first."[52]

In other words: These doors opened by Pierre are just the opportunities that will see us through – although he won't be there to witness as much.

But Pierre knew what change was afoot could hardly be ascribed to a single partner's unexpected expiry. Pierre's very customers were no longer making choices based on the system by which he'd reached the heights of his industry, he thought. The qualities that had been considered his strengths in the past were perhaps even held against him beyond the year 2000.

"Most of my clients had been bought by financiers who'd prohibited risk-taking," he says today. "However, without risk, there is no success – success being the dividend of risk.

"The choice of perfumes was devolved to the marketing (department), which was wary of the small companies of suppliers and intended to charge for market tests."

As it turns out, Dale Dewey, who'd sold NPD a fragrance market-testing firm, had indeed seen the future, even if his following venture, Jasmin.com, the Amazon of perfume, failed to come off – even though he lionized Bourdon, in fact.

There were many such odd juxtapositions – a generation of perfumery folks whose reverence of Bourdon hadn't forestalled their pursuit of ways and means of developing scents he either detested or, as part of a small firm, simply couldn't afford. This included the rise of Core Lists, which fragrance firms used to extort concessions on pricing. Don't grant big discounts and you might never be privy to a company's briefs again.

"Very quickly, I felt that the young people in the marketing teams did not like me," Pierre recalls. "I made them uncomfortable and I had the impression that they feared that an old nag like me would discover their level of incompetence in the raw materials of perfume. In fact, not having made the effort to learn the mysteries of the trade, they did not like perfumes and the smell bored them, when it made a Maurice Roger or a Forster jubilant."

And yet, Pierre was not embittered by this change – if change was even the right word for an epidemic of youth. Perhaps his enemy wasn't market-testing or core lists but time, always setting upon those most indisposed to change – repositories of wisdom hard-won – those least afraid of its consequences. Perhaps "naïve" was merely a synonym for "neuroplastic."

What mattered most to Pierre wasn't so much the dynamic, which has featured in every art and industry since the beginning of time, but whether he'd somehow slipped, almost overnight, from one side of the ledger to the other. It didn't take him long to draw a conclusion.

"In short," he told me, "I was on the way to becoming a has-been."

Pierre decided he would indeed bow out when he reached the earliest legal retirement age of 62, in 2008. Until then, he'd transmit his philosophies and techniques to a handful of students. To the perfumer-aspirants most able to benefit from his methods and likely to use them – maybe even develop them further.

But exactly whom? And what would an evolution of Pierre's work smell like? The answer would interest not just the teacher but the man who had for years milked him for his work. Who'd need a replacement for Pierre's basically-free formula submissions upon the perfumer's retirement.

Olivier Creed, naturally.

* * *

Olivier Creed found himself very suddenly, and at the same time as Pierre, confronting youth in his meetings due to unfortunate circumstance...only Olivier might have been responsible for instigating the generational tumult he thereafter had to abide. And he might have averted it finally with a different choice.

It began with Olivier's perfume business in America falling apart. Until the early Aughts, he'd had a single person responsible for distribution and publicity in the States, a short, feisty, half-Lebanese, half-French woman named Laurice Rahme, who'd previously worked for L'Oréal and for niche brand Annick Goutal and whose official title was CEO of Creed USA.

But that title doesn't fully convey her duties. She was a realizer of fragrance fantasies – a person who took Olivier's craziest claims and campaigned unwaveringly to have them featured in press clippings around the world.

It was she who hosted the Jasmin.com launch party in the Creed shop in New York, in a NoHo bazaar off Bleecker, at 9 Bond Street. It was she who had Creed customers ferried about in a 1967 Austin Princess, which she'd purchased from Cooper Classic Cars on Perry Street. It was she who scored Olivier profiles in the New York Observer and the New York Times.

But then Olivier dumped a bunch of Creed stock into the Middle East grey market because it wasn't selling at retail price after the turn of the Millennium – or sometime around 2003, as Pierre Bourdon's father lay dying – depressing the value of Laurice's unsold Creed bottles.

Or in an alternate telling by Laurice, Creed was resentful that Laurice had started her own perfume brand – Bond No. 9, named after the shop – and was selling it alongside his.

Either way, in the spring of 2004, she took out an ad in Women's Wear Daily that read, "Clear the way. Creed fragrances' liquidation sale 50 percent off. (Cheaper than the Internet.)"

(This would have pissed off Dale Dewey of Jasmin.com, too, if Dale's site hadn't fallen victim to the dotcom bubble-burst already – but it had.)

Laurice then proceeded to sell off all her Creed bottles. Just like that.

Olivier Creed announced he was suing her in French court, that she owed him a million bucks for inventory she'd acquired and for which she'd yet to pay. Laurice said she was going to seek damages against Creed in excess of what she owed.

Olivier said she had never given him a chance to buy the bottles she'd gotten rid of so damn easily.

"Our liquidation sale is absolutely permitted based on our contract," Laurice replied.

Ultimately, no actual lawsuits were ever filed. How could they have been? Olivier Creed would have to call to court a woman in possession of more than just his stories but the world's displeased retorts:

Laurice told me that, though she didn't publicize it in the Aughts, she had received piles of legal notices from royal families, including reps for Prince Charles and Prince Rainier, demanding that Olivier cease naming them as clients.

"I believed it," Laurice tells me today, of Olivier's initial talk of being a perfumer to sovereigns and celebrities. "To me, I had no reason to not believe it. It's only after the [legal notices] that I got – to stop using this and that, that they don't know who he is. Until then, I really never knew that he was lying."

Olivier's final word on Laurice, in 2005: "I really can't talk about her. But if I could, I would only have very bad things to say."[53]

It's hard to buy the idea even for a moment that Olivier was the aggrieved party in any dispute. But once his tie to Laurice was broken, once the continued operation of his US business was put in real jeopardy, culpability in the episode ceased to matter. He had a chance to prove his business bona fides at a perilous moment, no matter his shady ethical record.

And Olivier was faced with a specific choice, the resolution of which would either vault him higher in the tremendous US market or see him collapse altogether: Hire a distributor whose age and ideas more or less matched his own or bring into the fold a youthful executive, who could address the American market with a greater sense of local trends.

Except, rather shrewdly, Olivier realized he didn't have to choose at all — that one particular arrangement bridged this divide: He would hire not an individual but a family. A multigenerational family.

Their name was the Saujets. The father, Claude, who lived in Paris, had previously run the perfume business of Van Cleef & Arpels and the entire beauty division of pharmaceutical company Sanofi. Since being booted out of the latter in 1994, he'd licensed the Japanese brand Hanae Mori and had perfumes produced under that marque.

His sons were Emmanuel and Thomas, who'd grown up in the States and had worked with him to create the Hanae Mori line. These brothers were just 36 and 28 in 2004, when Olivier and Laurice fell out. But they offered the US knowledge Creed sought — they'd both attended Tufts and lived in New York — and their callowness was nullified, perhaps exceeded, by their father's vast experience.

Or so it seemed.

The Saujet brothers – working out of New York, their father still in Paris – issued their first press release for a new Creed fragrance in September 2004, or just months after Laurice left the picture. That it was forgettable entirely would soon seem to its great benefit – because the Saujet brothers, however well-intentioned, were about to begin a campaign whose execution was stymied from the start by their incapacity to speak ingenuously – to sound anything but unguent and gross.

Their idea, though an obvious PR stunt, was not a bad one, per se. In the wake of Olivier's public breakup with Laurice, the brothers sought to portray the Creed company as enlightened, magnanimous, charitable.

In 2005, Emmanuel Saujet told USA Today that Creed had donated front-row seats at Carnegie Hall to an auction (no word on the actual performance these tickets were for or the beneficiary holding the auction).

"Even as one enjoys luxury, such as a fine fragrance or an exceptional concert, one must also serve humanity," Emmanuel said, as though he were a schoolboy crafting his future Nobel Prize speech for homework.

The following May, the Saujets' press release announcing the donation of a perfume – Zeste Mandarine Pamplemousse – to injured members of the armed forces at Walter Reed Medical Center was so off-putting Gawker ran it under the headline, "What Wounded Soldier Doesn't Want to Smell Zesty?"[54]

These lines from the actual release, a boast to the media about the significance of the offering, composed in the dull, declarative sentences – in the naïve style – of the aforementioned fourth-grade dreamer:

"Creed is sending 260 bottles to Walter Reed Army Medical Center because there are 260 beds there. 260 bottles is a large quantity for Creed because all Creed fragrances are made – and bottled — by hand."

Gawker's commentary: "Today in horribly misguided, borderline-offensive press releases and swag stunts...Because if you can't have the bottom half of your leg back, Zeste Mandarine Pamplemousse is a decent replacement."

The bungled philanthropic effort didn't end with this hospital donation, however – nor did Gawker's accurate takedown spur the brothers to less overtly abominable oratory.

Three years later, in 2009, the Saujets published on the Creed Web site an article about the company's work with the US military that so bizarrely elevates the brand over the soldier it describes, it reads like an admission of guilt – *Hey, you got us, we don't give a fuck about charity so much as utilizing it to sell more stuff.*

The article:

It's obvious that Creed leather kits, hand-stitched in France from Italian leather, are an attractive take-anywhere way to store shaving gear, shampoo, soap and, of course, fragrance. But how strong and durable are they? Tough enough for U.S. troops serving in Iraq.

In 2009, as part of our regular shipments of grooming goods, including soaps and hair-and-body washes, to U.S. troops serving in Iraq, Creed sent a leather travel-grooming kit to U.S. Army First Lieutenant Anthony Arellano, serving in a field artillery unit outside the city of Tikrit. Lieutenant Arellano kept his Creed kit with him for the rest of his tour in Iraq, which included many dangerous missions. Creed is proud the kit withstood searing heat and sun, rough travel, sand and sustained use in perfect condition. Creed is very pleased that Lieutenant Arellano and his kit have returned safely to the U.S.

From its durable handle to its double-zip compartments, Creed kits sized at 10 inches long, six and one half inches high and four inches wide are an ideal way to carry with you all your grooming goods — wherever in the world you go.

Yes, that's real.

Worse, what you can't see in book form is that the first mention of the leather Dopp kit is a hyperlink to the page where one can purchase the item. Naturally.

This copy is bonkers – it's like someone particle-smashed at CERN the contents of "Catch-22" and a Hammacher Schlemmer catalog.

But it wasn't just the appearance of these gestures that was questionable – it was also the substance – the truth about the Saujets' supposed gifts.

In 2006, when Creed launched Original Santal, the Saujet brothers claimed the company was contributing a portion of its sales to the United Nations High Commission for Refugees. In 2008, they pledged revenue from the sale of a new women's perfume, Love in Black, to the World Wildlife Fund. Finally, in 2010, they offered a slice of sales from a new masculine scent, Aventus, to American Rivers, an environmental group.

The ultimate size of these donations – whether $5 or $5,000 or $50,000 – was never disclosed – while the promise to make them was most included in the Saujets' press releases and the Women's Wear Daily articles that covered them.

In 2020, a decade after the soldier-soap piece was posted online, I contacted American Rivers to ask about the donation from the proceeds of Aventus. They took some time to look at their records, before replying they couldn't find any gift related to Creed or Aventus. I then emailed Creed's US communications team (the Saujet brothers' underlings) about the American Rivers pledge.

"We've never heard of this donation but will look into this and get back to you," they said. They never did.

In 2021, I asked Creed's new London-based marketing chief about these supposed contributions – to a UN agency, to the WWF, to American Rivers. He didn't reply. But American Rivers maintains a list of donations in a directory used by fundraisers and accountants at nonprofits — and, perhaps more germane here, those who audit such institutions.

I checked it from 2010-2015 – or, for the first five years following Aventus' release. There's no mention of Creed, the Saujets, their company ICP – *nada*.

Which isn't to say the Saujet brothers are stingy people (perhaps fibbers, but not stingy). The company they run to handle Creed's business – International Cosmetics & Perfumes – gave money between

2009 and 2019 to the Girl Scouts; Women in Need, a critical care service for the homeless; and the French American School of New York.

The largest of those gifts, to the women's group, was between $5,000 and $9,999 – the size of which – however small compared to their overall wealth – isn't at all my focus. Who am I to sneer at a four-figure sum?

I'm just reciting what else is visible in the public records, including nonprofit tax forms, and wondering why apportionments from actual Creed revenue are nowhere mentioned or made known – as if there's reason for them be buried.

For instance, also visible: In just two years, 2017 and 2018, their family foundation gave a combined $15,000 to the brothers' alma mater, Tufts and a large donation to Convenant House. And Emmanuel Saujet has personally given money to the National Resources Defense Council and Bill Clinton's foundation.

Meanwhile, some of these Creed fragrances introduced since the Saujets took over the business in North America have raked in incredible sums of cash.

In fact, that's perhaps the most amazing part of Olivier Creed's succession plan. These ineloquent, confused kids he hired were never hindered by their obvious weaknesses – not if one judges them by the sales expansion concurrent to their tenure. In 2010, Women's Wear Daily said Creed sales volume had hit $20 million in the US, or triple the figure at their hiring in 2004.[55]

If this seems a small figure for a company at the heart of a book, I don't disagree. Nor do I believe the brothers played much of a role in reaching that sum – it was the juice, some of it still produced by Pierre, of course. Original Santal – the fragrance the Saujets introduced in 2006 by pledging money to a UN agency? Pierre believes it was his losing brief for a Jil Sander Sun fragrance of the early Aughts (I say "believes" because there are some fragrances he knows he formulated but whose starting point he no longer recalls – such as Creed Erolfa, of 1992, also his own composition, though the brief for which it was rejected escapes him presently).

But that these bumbling Saujet brothers helped bring the company to the 2010 calendar year is vitally important. For it's then that Creed's sales surged incredibly, drawing the eye of private equity investors, who'd ultimately pay nearly a billion dollars for the firm. And it was in 2010, too, that Creed released what some consider the best men's scent ever made – and certainly the masculine fragrance most copied and imitated the world ever this century.

This is the male fragrance mentioned at the top of the chapter, a vintage 2011 4 oz. bottle of which was put up for sale on eBay in autumn 2020, amidst a pandemic, for $50,000 (plus $4.75 in shipping).

Its name, by now far too familiar to perfumistas and fragheads, is Creed Aventus. And although Pierre Bourdon had officially retired about three years before its release, he had as much of a hand in it as anyone.

This is the story of a genius' last students and the most copied scent in the world. And how, having insinuated himself into the life of their teacher, a hustler named Olivier attempted to slide into the pupils' sphere.

To extract one or two more blockbuster formulas for nothing (or something close to that).

And how he – utterly evading karma – *succeeded*.

Chapter 12: The Student

The years were not unkind to Pierre Bourdon's body, but they were also not inevident.

His greyed hair – parted on the left side of his scalp, the bulk of it combed over to the right – had grown hard and thin, its former bounce, the silky resilience of its earliest days, that period during which he'd lost his virginity on the begrimed floor of a maid's room, long gone.

His eyes had always radiated either profound excitement or deep disgust – either they opened wide as if to seduce you whole, to swallow you up, body-and-soul, gleefully and with your consent – or they seemed themselves standoffish – deeper set in his skull than you remembered, unblinking and black, cold beads on the floor of a frigid river, unreachable first and impenetrable on top of that.

But now those eyes, while still capable of such contradictory appearance, were also ringed by thin radial lines, wrinkles spreading from the outside corners of his peepers toward his cheek bones and ears, like a child's depiction of the rays of the sun. Actually, Pierre's lines, too, lent the circles from which they emanated a kind of energy and goodwill. As if he were bursting yet with great ideas and bonhomie for all who'd help him realize them.

But then there was his beard – an unruly grey bush streaked with white, neither red nor patchy but nevertheless evocative of Van Gogh's in its wildness, for the artistic statement it made (intentionally or not) – a thick, rustic shag over his cheeks and lips and chin.

And what of that statement? Was this semi-trimmed, half-restrained beard meant to be read as defiant? And if so, a challenge of what or whom? Was this more broadly his version of not going gentle into that good night? Or was the wildness a concession to his eventual demise – a first step toward the dusty and decayed state that is our common destiny?

All of the above, I believe. And which of these qualities came first depended on his mood at that moment – and of late, business having become turbulent, his mind had become a somewhat darker and more volatile place.

Pierre already knew he was being pushed out of the perfumery – Fragrance Resources – he'd essentially co-founded.

He sensed it not just from the increasingly youthful and risk-averse clients of the firm but by the commissions he was receiving. Sure, in casting his lot with a smaller company, he'd a decade earlier resigned himself to receiving more minor briefs, for insignificant brands such as Van Gils, Marc O'Polo, and Ghost – he couldn't complain about that plight, especially as he'd had offers over the years from all the big companies – to return to Roure, to jump ship to Firmenich.

"If my life had to be remade, I wouldn't change a thing, even if it could have been more glorious if I had stayed in what you call 'the petrol houses,'" he told me, referencing my quite unintentional nickname for Givaudan and Firmenich and IFF in our correspondence (I'd meant to call them "oil houses").

"I would have signed more perfumes," Pierre added, "but I would have been more unhappy there. Having had my fill of it from my father, I am resistant to authority, except that, legitimate, exercised by men I admire."

But even if Pierre maintained his equanimity during the Aughts, or claims to have, one feels frustrated for him and what he endured during that period all the same. Because just as Olivier Creed had to suffer the boneheaded philanthropic blabber of the Saujet brothers, Pierre had to tolerate the most bizarre clients – a procession of carnival barkers whose proposals, unreflective of Pierre's accomplishments, I construe as insulting years after the fact (though Pierre told me he was okay with it all).

Take the 2004 scent Francesco Smalto FullChoke. The men's clothier of that name, Smalto, who'd licensed his marque to a perfume company, had been convicted nine years earlier of "aggravated pimping" for providing prostitutes to the dictator of Gabon in return for the purchase of tailored clothing.

And then there was the creative director on the project, Franck Boclet, who not only insisted on a glass dildo bottle for the juice but the allusion to fellatio for the juice's name.

By 2004, Pierre was looking ahead anyway. He knew he was nearly finished for reasons entirely unrelated to the crystal cock container. Perfumery is no place for old men. It mercilessly spits out even its most accomplished practitioners once they start losing briefs.

The only possible way for Pierre Bourdon to continue onward was to teach a few students, pass on his ideas. Perhaps another perfumer might have had to search for such disciples – but in Pierre's case it was his own work of 15 years prior that yielded his most consequential mentee.

See, when Pierre first opened the Paris office of Takasago, one of his few employees was a manager of the company's factory. Pierre liked this guy so much he took him along when Pierre left to join Fragrance Resources.

This manager, thusly having access to all the raw materials and compounded perfumes in Pierre's workplace, took home one day one of the latter items – Pierre's creation for Joop! Homme – as a present for his son.

"The first time I smelled the perfume, I felt an emotion that I never felt before," Jean-Christophe Herault, then the factory manager's son, told me. "But I didn't understand really why." Nor did he know the identity of its creator.

Herault was nevertheless intrigued by its potential – if he liked it so profoundly, what would others think? And so he wore it and those near him took notice in school. "It smells so good – what is it?'" he was asked. Girls even stopped him in the street to say coquettishly, "It fits you very well."

Herault decided this was to be the perfume of his life – but that wasn't the only decision he made on the occasion. He began to smell everything. Perfume, food, plants, paper, wood, air. Not that he'd decided to become a perfumer yet – he went off to university to study chemistry with no clear idea about his desired profession. But Joop set him sniffing.

It was only after he left university that his dad suggested Herault join him in the Fragrance Resources factory, in the quality control lab, where he'd be able to smell all the raw materials that make up a perfume and work with the gas chromatography equipment – aka the GC-MS machines that break down ingredients, molecules, perfumes into their constituent parts.

"I began to understand that in bergamot oil you have linalyl acetate and you have the same thing in lavender," he told me. "In the beginning that sounds a little bit strange."

Increasingly able to accommodate the odd notions intrinsic to perfumery – delighting in their study –Herault felt finally confident enough to approach Pierre. No small feat. Pierre was handsome, tanned, purposeful in his motions – standoffish to those whom he'd no desire to stand near, his gaze penetrating when interrogating the obviously simpleminded.

Herault was a looser goose – a willowy, overgrown boy. His sandy hair, thinning out and receded, perpetually looked tousled, even when he slicked it back. His eyes bulged, as if to indicate his curiosity about the seductive field in which he found himself, yet his eyelids drooped – heavy curtains midway closed, as though the man-boy hadn't slept well in years. An active adolescent's Visine-deserving eyes on the morning after. His nose, too, was self-contradictory – doorknob-protuberant, as though he'd been cuffed by the cool kids, but also more promisingly prominent, as if to indicate a focus, his willingness to be led by his sense of smell down any path or alley.

He might've passed for a magician with such contradictory, merely half-mature qualities. He wore Lacoste shirts that seemed slightly schlumpy on him in spite of their quality and fit.

"You know, Pierre, I have a dream," Herault recalls saying. "I would like to become a perfumer myself. I've smelled a lot of ingredients, a lot of the production. I analyzed the chromatography. I'm very passionate. I've discovered a lot of stuff in this world. I'm really fascinated."

He then repeated himself, before popping the big question: "I think I would like to become a perfumer. Could you give me some tips on how I could enter the Givaudan perfumery school?"

This was, of course, Pierre's alma mater (in the '90s the name was changed from Roure to Givaudan after a merger of two corporate siblings).

Pierre's answer?

"No."

Herault was stunned for the briefest of moments, perhaps a nanosecond. Then Pierre kept going.

"I'm gonna train you," he told Herault.

"Pierre is super talented and super smart," Herault thought. "He knows history, literature, art. He speaks with tremendous eloquence.

He's the kind of guy you can listen to speak for hours and hours about any subject, because he has always a very interesting point of view."

"Holy hell," Herult concluded. "This is the opportunity of my life."

He was right – but only in the bigger picture. Pierre asked for a few months to concentrate on his own affairs – then, those months became a few years. During the wait, Pierre urged Herault to head to Grasse to smell all the flowers one can't find in the north – where Herault lived after his parents split, an hour outside of Paris – including Grasse's jasmine, rose, tuberose.

Bourdon exhorted Herault to sniff even the leaves — "because the leaves can have an odor, too."

Finally, in 2000, Pierre called Herault back to Paris.

"You have to come visit me," Pierre said. "We are going to sign a contract."

"I thought it was the kind of contract that (stipulates) when your training is over, you have to spend a few years in the company to bring back to the company what the company gave you," Herault recalls.

Pierre took Herault to a fancy restaurant.

"This is something you have to appreciate also," Pierre said with regard to the food and drink, "because perfumery is very linked to flavor." After the two men polished off their first bottle of wine, Pierre got down to business.

"As for the contract," he said, "you are going to read 'À la recherche du temps perdu.' It's a novel by Marcel Proust. If you won't read it, I am not going to train you."

You can picture Herault, having toiled for years in the Grasse heat analyzing flowers and leaves per Pierre's request, momentarily crestfallen at what seemed until just then a celebratory dinner. He was not being asked to join the company for proper training but to read seven thick, dense volumes about Swann and madeleines.

Of course, if he was upset or deterred, he didn't give voice to those feelings. Nor did he even try to protest. He signed the contract and then set off to fulfill his end of it. A year later, he'd read Proust's entire masterpiece – and obtained an understanding of the assignment in the first place – so much so that he began studying art history to supplement his literary deep dive, to provide a further artistic element, or source of material, for to his future perfumery.

"Step by step you can see how Proust himself decided to become an artist, a writer," Herault told me of "La Recherche." You learn that artists take inspiration from other artists – and from nature, emotions.

"And you can see step by step how the novel is building itself. At the end when you finish, you say, But in fact, I saw with my eyes the creation of the novel itself while reading it!"

This was Herault's takeaway – "La Recherche" takes its very construction as its subject. And if the book can show you the how its story came to be, it can serve, too, as a more general guide to artistic endeavor.

Bourdon was pleased Herault understood the rationale for his curriculum, and after a few discussions about art further, Pierre finally and officially welcomed Herault to the company Fragrance Resources – where the student began conventional training.

Although Pierre's style, of perfumery and pedagogy, was not necessarily conventional. Always two opposite forces tugged at the students: Pierre stressed fundamental structures and the rigorous refinement of accords but also the embedding within these templates of ideas ambitious and fanciful.

Perhaps his own Cool Water is an instructive example: Pierre spent a decade building the thing from the endpoint of prior classics – but only so that, within that particular envelope, he could go all out with the aquatic vibe, the overdose of dihydromyrcenol. And thusly Pierre instructed his student: to master classic perfume structure so that any new accords inserted therein would then pop – so that a dynamic tension in the juice would keep customers coming back again and again to sniff out the taut balance, the relationship between erudite accords and undeniable imagination.

In total, Herault wound up training to be a perfumer for 8 years.

* * *

What was Pierre up to while Herault smelt flowers in Grasse – what work consumed him such that he couldn't yet begin to help Herault? Wasn't he merely working on cheap scents?

Sorta.

But Pierre was doing something quite consistently with his formulas, even if it escaped the attention of his clients and industry peers – he was working constantly with a pineapple top note, as if in possession of a larger idea whose first principle required that fruit's chemical evocation.

Even when he didn't realize it, Pierre was a perfumer in search of certain singularities – the most bestial fragrance (Kouros), the most aquatic (Cool Water) and now, perhaps, the most handsome, the best-constructed fresh cologne (never mind his clients' tremendously tight budgets).

A list of his post-Y2K scents featuring pineapple up top:

Francesco Smalto FullChoke

Ferre

Ferre for Men

Ferre Bluemusk

Cabaret Homme by Gres

The Brun — Jean Charles Brosseau

Montblanc Individuel

Man by Judith Williams

Lobogal pour Lui

Ambre Topkapi, Parfums MDCI
Basic Instinct by Van Gils
Escada Magnetism
Courtesan by Worth
D for Luciano Soprani

This is not to say Pierre was the first to propound such a construction. The perfume critic and professor of quantum bioscience Luca Turin provided me historical context via email:

"The butyric esters and the green-pineapple note of allyl amyl glycolate go all the way back to the '20s, and Patou's Colony, so Bourdon (may he be blessed) is following a long tradition."

Pierre's fixation on the pineapple note, perhaps grounded in the history Luca shared, ensured not only his work's connection to the past but the survival of its tenets in the future. Because now, in the present, Herault was watching him.

In the '80s, Pierre had sought to quadruple the amount of pineapple – the galbex and allyl amyl glycolate – found in Drakkar Noir in order to make Cool Water.

Twenty years later, Pierre's student, Herault, upon arriving in the office, watched his teacher employ notable pineapple doses – almost as if it was Pierre's parting manifesto, his valedictory lesson to subsequent generations:

The best scents begin here, with pineapple.

In fact, the one fragrance Pierre and Herault co-authored – Canali for Men of 2005 – features a pineapple top note. And this release itself was a passing of the baton from the legend to the lad – because by the admission of both parties, Herault created 95 percent of the scent and Pierre was simply brought on to finish and sign it so the Italian client could brag about its legendary author.

"It is true that I have always had an appetite for pineapple notes since their use in Drakkar Noir and in Aliage, pioneering fragrances in this regard," Pierre told me later. "They have a salivating aspect and bring an unusual and frankly modern color to the compositions.

"That Jean-Christophe Hérault was influenced by my style is likely and quite natural," Pierre added. "I myself was inspired by that of my master, Edmond Roudnitska, for Féminité du Bois, in particular, which contains the spices of (Roudnitska's) Eau d'Hermès."

And so, having contributed his lot to the evolution of perfume, the man bade adieu. It's unclear exactly when – some day between Pierre's co-signing of the Canali fragrance to please the Italian client and the year 2010 – a momentous one for reasons to be explained momentarily – he finally called it quits and began letting others know.

One such man was Olivier Creed, of course, who was supposed to pay Pierre that day a major, many-digit lump sum for all the formulas Pierre had ghostwritten – the perfumer having received until now just tailored suits for his trouble.

But Olivier declined to pay – almost as if Pierre had been a fool for ever believing he would.

"I must confess that I felt a certain bitterness for having been shamelessly exploited by this guy – whose actions Kathy always reproached me for allowing, whom she disapproved of," Pierre told me. "I should have listened to her!"

Kathy Bourdon, who'd always urged her husband not to turn over papers to this suave and insidious tailor-heir: "As far as Creed is concerned, that he appropriated the authorship of the perfumes of Pierre or others who provided him (formulas), it's fair game… Pierre and the other perfumers Creed worked with knew what to expect."

She added, regarding Pierre's willingness to part with such valuable IP: "He is not the only one and will surely not be the last to do so."

Obviously, he wasn't – because Olivier Creed is incorrigible – unstintingly sneaky, in possession of unparalleled chutzpah – and because perfumers, always fighting for the slightest bit of notice, will sacrifice their dignity in its pursuit.

Once Pierre left the Fragrance Resources building, Olivier Creed waltzed in in search of a new ghostwriter who'd be able to pick up where Pierre left off. Naturally, that meant a visit to Jean-Christophe Herault, Bourdon's most notable student at the time but also his most vulnerable.[56]

Yes, Herault had trained alongside Pierre, but this heterodox education – instead of years-long training at the Givaudan school or ISIPCA in Versailles – might make recruiters at the multinationals – Givaudan, Firmenich, IFF – wary. His education had been a calculated risk.

Now he needed to prove it had worked. And so Olivier entered Herault's workspace with an intention to manipulate the man, to take advantage of his uncertain status in the trade.

"I worked a lot with Pierre Bourdon," Olivier said, "and Pierre Bourdon is today retired. You are still in Fragrance Resources. Could you do a new masculine perfume?"

"Thank you for thinking about me," Herault replied. "I'm very pleased."

Then Olivier showed the young perfumer a musk whose name I've promised a source not to name – but whose nature I can. It was an alicyclic musk – that is, a musk containing a carbon ring with an offshoot tail that to my chemically-illiterate – and perhaps overly libidinous – mind resembles sperm – that had only first been synthesized in the 1990s.

That date helped to make the musk special: it had been a captive (protected intellectual property) of a single firm for decades and, therefore, had not been widely used – was not already the subject of extensive perfumer experimentation.

Moreover, it's possible Olivier didn't bring this musk but an enantiomer – the same compound but a version rotated either clockwise (a dextro-rotation) or counterclockwise (a levo-rotation) – such small tilts sometimes having a remarkable impact on an ingredient's properties, aroma included.

Whichever Olivier offered up to Herault, he was sharing a singular material – one whose fresh, warm, fruity nature both comforted and aroused. An ingredient as soft and reassuring as your partner's favorite t-shirt – the one you co-opt come pajama-time – and as juicy and inebriating as a cocktail – that dancehall drink shared by strangers soon not to be.

A heady, hormonal, playful musk indeed.

And so Olivier – the world's greatest fragrance-evaluator, a hero if only he'd settled for that title – told Christophe Herault:

The musk here smells so good it is already a fragrance in and of itself.

Herault, considering this notion, as yet unfamiliar with this new musk's facets, realized Olivier's approach provided him tremendous opportunity.

Okay, I can create a perfume with this musk, Herault said, finally. *But the thing is, as you dig the musk, so do I go gaga for ambery ingredients – and one in particular – ambroxan.* I will work with your infatuation so long as you accommodate mine. *The fragrance at its core will be ambroxan ensconced in this musk.*

Olivier agreed to that compromise (he was once again getting a talented youngster to apply himself for the sake of the Creed business – he was hardly in a position to complain or inclined to do so).

Herault began in the lab with that basic amber-musk combo – and was, by his own account, completely blown away.

"It smelled so good," he told me, as if savoring still that first whiff. "It was already the starting point of Aventus."

That's how Jean-Christophe Herault agreed with Olivier Creed to create for the latter the most successful niche perfume of all time. Easy-peasy. As though Olivier hadn't screwed over the teacher of whom Herault was so fond.

But Pierre Bourdon was not offended. He knew the industry was in the midst of tremendous consolidation. Quest had been bought by Givaudan. It was only a matter of time before tiny Fragrance Resources would meet the same fate (it would later be bought by IFF, in fact).

Pierre could not begrudge the kid this survivalism.

Actually, to some degree Pierre was personally responsible for Aventus and the ample riches it brought Olivier.

Recall that 2005 Canali fragrance co-signed by Pierre and Herault? Well, it contained pineapple and musk and jasmine, all ingredients Herault later used in Aventus – the pineapple having been a Bourdon signature for years, as abovementioned. If Pierre should get credit for anything, it was Herault's instinct to top off this new Creed juice with pineapple. But that was 2010.

In 2009, a year before Aventus came to market, Herault created Canali dal 1934, an evolution of that first Canali scent whose ingredients so closely mirror those found in the Creed it could be called Neanderthalic Aventus: the two share notes of pineapple, blackcurrant, musk, ambergris.

The only major distinction, aside from the quality of the raw materials and the unfortunate use of nutmeg in the Canali, is the base – Aventus' combination of a captive alicyclic musk and ambroxan, the result of the Olivier-Herault compromise (you put in your favorite material and I will mine).

One of the first things I mentioned to Herault during our pandemic video chat:

"Canali dal 1934," I said, "this one has a lot of the elements that you see a year later in Aventus."

"You're right," Herault said. "You're totally right."

A Creed insider with knowledge of this overlap told me, of Olivier Creed: "One thing is certain – he owes *absolutely everything* to Pierre."

Which isn't to take away from the efforts made by Herault and

Olivier, even if they were enabled by Pierre's earlier work and pedagogy, utterly informed by his philosophy and technique – because Aventus is fruity-woody-musky seduction. An achievement artistic and financial both.

Olivier Creed was absolutely right – the musk he conveyed to Herault is a brilliant raw material and a better starting point – one of the few musks that can serve as a top and base note both, such that it winds up saturating itself – steeping in its own juices. A batch that seems too woody at first can, over time, develop an ineffable sensuousness merely from macerating in that musk.

But there's so much more – Aventus manages to check off all the most desirable boxes. There's a mouth-watering brightness to its Bourdon-ian pineapple opening. It features a rejuvenating, summery citrus in its bergamot – and a kind of dignified-yet-playful fruitiness from its apple and blackcurrant.

The smoky birch – only a distant relation of that same ingredient as used in classic and unrelenting leather chypres of the past, such as Knize Ten and Bel Ami – nevertheless combines with the patchouli to pack a minor-note, unexpected gut-punch, a leathery substantiality not apparent at first whiff but without which Aventus would just be another bright and cooling cologne *et rien de plus*.

Similarly, just enough vanilla exists in the mix for me to imagine running my hand along the perimeter of a cake and sucking its frosting off my fingers. There's a concession here to our implacable desire for just-prepared pastry – but only to a degree. It induces you to want a great deal more but doesn't indulge you that vice.

And of course, all these aromatic ingredients outstrip what's put into most bottles because Olivier really does spend heavily – having always taken Pierre's formulas and inserted for each ingredient listed the most expensive version on the market.

Aventus was no different – Olivier made the same costly replacements for Herault's recipe. The result was fragrant – and financial – history. And it was perhaps to acknowledge as much that Olivier called Herault a few years into Aventus' rise up the sales charts and invited him to a fancy dinner.

That Olivier never remunerated Pierre was shameful – but now at least, Olivier had the opportunity to do better by his accomplished successor.

How would this dinner go – what would Olivier actually say?

Chapter 13: The Masterpiece

Aventus had been projected to take in $5 million in its first year of sales.[57] But it very quickly garnered a reputation as the ultimate lady-killer (yes, that sounds sexist to my ear, but this was the language often used; I'm merely playing messenger).

"Baffled by how Creed Aventus is such a compliment-getter," posted one user on the perfume forum Basenotes, in 2012. "Doesn't matter," wrote another with a demeaning penchant for the majuscule "W": "It's just like a Woman. Don't try to understand her. Just love her."

And the male frag-buying populace was a much more potent demographic than you might think. For the year ending in the summer of 2019, prestige perfume sales were up 5 percent – due entirely to men buying more high-end scents, women's sales having stalled.

The world's foremost fragrance critic, Luca Turin, gave Aventus four of four stars.

There were huge debates all over Reddit, Fragrantica, Basenotes, Instagram about the best batches every year (about one batch per month was released). I've personally owned, swapped and sold batches with friends and strangers for the last half-decade.

The Business of Fashion trade publication called the juice the "Supreme of the Fragrance World" in a headline. The prices were certainly in line with that too-cool-for-school clothing brand: $140 for an ounce, $240 for 2.5 oz, $280 for 4 oz.

(Today 3.3 oz costs $435.)

By 2017, Aventus was the best-selling fragrance in Neiman Marcus. It was also supposedly such a big hit at Bloomingdales in NY that when the store ran out of Aventus in the week leading up to Father's Day, fans waited and instead purchased it *after* the holiday, once the shelves were restocked. On the Friday *after* Father's Day 2017, Bloomies sold $11,800 of Aventus.

By 2019, Aventus represented 40 percent of all Creed sales. By that same point, the company was taking in $190 million in revenue every year.[58] By the time Olivier sold Creed in 2020, it was a company with annual revenue of $200-270 million and a private valuation of nearly $1 billion.

That means yearly Aventus sales had reached $80 million – at the very least.

And its formula, for being so utterly pervaded with fine naturals and Firmenich captives, wouldn't yield its fullest magic to even the cleverest of copycats. Not that such difficulties stopped them from trying. Aventus became the most cloned and influential scent of a globalized fragrance era, of the century.

In the United States, the most popular men's eau de parfum sold on Amazon became Armaf Club de Nuit Intense Man, a screechy-loud Aventus dupe (which was, perhaps counter to what you may think about knockoffs, actually produced by a perfumer at the smaller French fragrance firm Mane; it's how Mane and Robertet and Sozio, these smaller but no-less-legit-for-being-so firms, stay in business, partly: clones).

A brief look at some of the other attempted Aventus copies that came to market:

From the United Arab Emirates: Afnan Supremacy Silver, Ajmal Amaze, Reyane Insurrection II Pure, Armaf Bucephalus XI, Rasasi

9325 Pour Lui (aka Rasasi Zebra), Al Haramain L'Aventure, Lattafa al Dur al Maknoon Silver, Swiss Arabian Shawq, Boadicea the Victorious Consort.

Hany Hafez of Alexandria Fragrances calls his version "Brasilia," Zara calls theirs "Vibrant Leather."

Luxury brands: The Orchid Man by Frapin, Mazzolari Nero, Pierre Guillaume Aqaysos, Floris London 1976, Jeroboam Vespero.

Western brands: Montblanc Explorer (made by Givaudan), Perry Ellis America, Bond No. 9 the Scent of Peace for Him, Abercrombie & Fitch Authentic Man.

Licensed car brands: Mercedes-Benz Select (made by Firmenich). Tonino Lamborghini Invicibile.

In New York, Morning Chess by Vilhelm Parfumerie.

In California, Cremo Bergamot & Musk.

In India, Projekt Alternative Alexa.

In Turkey, Nishane Hacivat (though Nishane's owners insisted to me Hacivat was not created to be a clone and doesn't even smell like one, and to be fair, it's probably the most Aventus-adjacent juice on this list) and Alghabra City of Jasmine (now, that's a straight-up clone).

In Saudi Arabia, Avenue by Al-Rehab.

In Italy, Lucevera Accendis and Tiziana Terenzi Orion.

In Spain, Loewe Escencia Pour Homme EDP.

In France, M. Micallef Royal Vintage, Mauboussin Discovery.

In England, Laboratory Perfumes Amber, Dunhill Desire Gold, No. 9 Victor Milton Lloyd, English Laundry London, Electimuss Imperium.

And then there are the countless releases whose inspiration, while likely encompassing a range of work, was primarily Aventus (perhaps even without the creators realizing as much).

"A few years ago, a perfumer told me, 'Have you noticed that in Sauvage from Dior, it's all the ingredients in Aventus?'" Jean-Christophe Herault recounted to me, namechecking a Dior that came out five years following the Creed. "I didn't realize. I smell it, and I recognize all the ingredients – you have everything (from Aventus). You have the patchouli. You have the musk. You have the isobutyl quinoline, the leather effects. You have everything.

"And I was very proud."

* * *

Olivier Creed invited Herault to dinner. Aventus was already a smash. In fact, Olivier had taken to wearing it himself.

To any outside observer, this would have seemed a significant rendezvous. Creed had clawed his way into the spotlight by playing Alain Delon in "Purple Noon" – had been ruthless in his manipulation and dismissal of others for personal gain.

To that point: Pierre was still heartbroken over the unpaid retirement money Olivier had promised and then refused to deliver. Olivier didn't seem to care in the least.

But now Olivier was treating Pierre's student to dinner, the meal itself possibly a platform for Olivier to announce a further gift.

Had time mellowed Olivier Creed – reduced his ego, such that he no longer felt it necessary to lie to the world, to claim an identity not his own?

Certainly, the years had begun to show in his figure and physiognomy, nearly 40 years after he'd first slipped into Pierre's office and the perfumer thought: *I don't like this guy sniffing all my work, but damn – he's a suave one, a cross in appearance between Sean Connery and Roger Moore.*

Now in his mid-70s, Olivier could be seen around town in the warmer months wearing linen button-down shirts, finely-creased seersucker pants, white leather loathers – bright white digs that, by virtue of their contrast to his ever-ruddier features, underscored a creeping anecdotage.

Those ruby cheeks, drooping further daily, had nearly become jowls. The skin beneath his eyes was both puffed up and papery-thin. His broad, bald pate – cowl-like over his visage – made his eyes seem darker and more deeply sunken than they actually were. Here and there he was pockmarked, his countenance undular if not outright craggy.

Time hadn't waited for him, despite his usurpation of others' lives, his commandeering of their stories. A fanciful imagination was no buffer against increasingly apparent finitude.

At some point in the meal, once pleasantries had passed between them, Olivier began:

"You know, it's such a success, I don't know how to thank you," he said. "That's why I'm going to treat you to dinner…but that's not enough."

Here, I imagine Olivier having taken in a big breath, as if he needed additional oxygen to speak sincerely.

"You can say that you are the creator of Aventus," he continued. "Because you *are* the creator. Even in magazines. You can say it to everybody."

A moment of silence.

If Herault wasn't completely stunned, he was, at the very least, greatly relieved.

Since producing Aventus, he'd barely told a soul of his authorship – to the point that even IFF, the firm he joined not long after finishing the Aventus formula, had no idea it was his composition. In fact, a colleague once asked him to produce an Aventus clone, under the assumption that Pierre Bourdon had produced Aventus and Pierre's student could best replicate that work.

Herault thanked Olivier greatly for the opportunity to publicize his creation of the scent. What a tremendous boost that would be to his burgeoning career, he continued.

Was Herault letting off Olivier too easily? Most assuredly.

But it wasn't in Herault's constitution to request anything at all – let alone an actual percentage of the profits, say, or some kind of sales-correlated bonus. A current colleague of his at IFF told me Herault is "afraid of his own shadow."

Nor does the industry appreciate independent-minded perfumers. These multinational firms will sooner side with the person purchasing raw materials than the creatives whose formulas call for their use.

If Herault had pressed Olivier for further payment – or even the right of first refusal to produce a future Creed scent –Olivier could have had him blacklisted at institutions more loyal to money than talent (Olivier's purchases of raw materials have made him a good many friends).

And Herault, by his own admission, had been particularly nervous about the whole ghostwriting arrangement from the jump.

"I was a little bit shy," he told me. He'd built a scent that had changed his industry, but any desire to say so was exceeded by a fear of the man who'd commissioned it. "I didn't want to fight Olivier Creed."

Now, Herault wouldn't have to – he could speak freely – including to me, a writer working on an entire book about the trade.

"I am not shy anymore," he insisted to me. "When someone talks to me about Aventus, I tell them I am the creator of Aventus."

This is where the Herault portion of this book should have ended – the man having earned a freedom of speech denied his mentor, the Creed universe of lies having come ultimately undone.

But Herault's story continued – and to understand why, one first has to rewind a single day. I spoke to Herault via Zoom on July 9, 2020. By incredible coincidence, just the night before, he'd dined with Olivier, this meal having been a product of the perfumer's initiative, a separate engagement entirely from the encounter above.

The pandemic was still particularly perilous for the elderly in those early July days. Herault hadn't seen Olivier for a long time, so he sent Olivier a text, to check in on him, make sure he was okay. Monsieur Creed was no longer "super young," in Herault's words. And when Olivier called him back, the two decided to dine together once more, this time to celebrate the 10th anniversary of Aventus' release (the first Aventus press release was issued on June 21, 2010 – my birthday, incidentally).

The next afternoon – maybe 16 hours after he dined with Olivier – I spoke to Herault, who, granted permission to proclaim himself Aventus inventor, no longer feared the powers that be, Olivier in particular.

And for a moment, I believed both Herault and Olivier changed men, even if something felt off, surreal, too easy. Olivier had spent four decades hiding what he perceived to be his own inadequacy (despite the fact that he was the best fragrance *evaluator* on the planet). Herault hadn't told any magazines about his blockbuster byline, despite having been granted that permission months earlier.

Was our Zoom call really the final word?

A day after our chat, I shot Herault an email thanking him for his stories and time and posing an additional question. Aventus was a gold mine – had Olivier briefed Herault on the two masculines Creed had released since – Viking and Aventus Cologne? Because, I figured, Herault had done so well on his first go, surely Olivier would have wanted to solicit his work again.

And also, could Herault introduce me to Pierre himself, whom I had yet to meet (but would eventually regardless)?

I received this odd, spare response six days later:

"Could you tell me a little more about your book? No, I don't work with Creed anymore. I haven't been briefed."

On Bourdon: "Unfortunately, there is nothing I can do for you.

Sorry."

These were the last two emails – the last sentences – I received from Herault, whom I attempted to contact again every which way, having gotten along with him splendidly for hours during our Zoom (and through a period of emailed correspondence in which I relayed to him every detail of the book I then knew long before he weirdly asked me what it was all about).

That bizarre shift in behavior in a man who celebrated repeatedly a newfound freedom to gab to reporters, myself included, provoked a few possible explanations among his colleagues, some of whom were by then my trusted confidants.

During his week of radio silence, BlackRock must've gotten to him, its long term private capital fund having bought Creed for close to a billion bucks in the spring – so went one theory (not necessarily my own). The finance folks perhaps didn't appreciate the spilling of secrets after such an investment. Their purchase of the company, while due mostly to the runaway sales of Aventus, was motivated in part by the mythology — stories of Creed's centuries-old techniques and unbroken father-son chain of fragrance expertise. How to sell that story when Herault's candor made plain the conceit and conceitedness?

Or perhaps his bosses at IFF, a publicly traded company, had gently chastised the man for breaking the industry code of Omerta – theory two.

But there's a third possibility, apart from Herault having found me a colossal ass and merely pretended to enjoy our dialogue from the start.

And that's simply that Olivier got to Herault the same way Olivier had gotten to Pierre – gotten into his head –had insinuated himself into the young man's life as he had the older one – by lurking around Herault, by promising him eventual riches, by asserting with his very presence, his attitude, his posh demeanor, a sort of aristocratic privilege, an entitlement not just to the work of others but to their thoughts.

It wouldn't surprise me if Herault, having spoken to Olivier just the night before our Zoom, checked in with Olivier a day or two after it, as well – to ensure he hadn't overstepped certain boundaries – even though Olivier had explicitly allowed such moves.

Perhaps Olivier knew all along Herault would never be confident enough to take advantage of this ostensible freedom. Maybe he figured Herault would tell one writer (it happened to be me) and then hide.

This gloss becomes more likely when you evaluate Olivier's other move during this period – because Herault was not the final student of Pierre's to be so targeted.

Olivier went after one final Bourdon-bred nose.

* * *

Julien Rasquinet had a surer touch than Herault, was not a boy at all but a handsome man with a head of curly hair and big bushy eyebrows. He wore sport coats above an unbuttoned oxford shirt whose collar was sometimes smushed, the rumpling only adding to a kind of dressed-up variation on boho chic.

Yet he came across as more gentleman than downtown gigolo, as the sort of grounded young man who'd absorbed only the best characteristics of the two contrasting worlds in which he had been raised – Paris and the Normandy countryside (Pierre's ancestral home region, too).

Just listen to him describe this upbringing with unaffected poetry:[59]

When I think of my childhood, what comes to my mind is the smell of Normandy. So many scent memories...the fresh cut grass, the rose garden, the Butterfly bushes, the smell of rotten apples on the ground in October, the wet soil in the forest in autumn, and the chimney fire in winter, the smell of

*my horse, and of the room where I hung her saddle, the smell of mint nearby
the river, and the smell of earth as I tended my vegetable garden when I was
11 years old.*

But like Herault, he had no perfumery diploma from the Givaudan
school or ISIPCA. Rasquinet was a former intern at IFF who'd decided
to go into business and gotten a degree in that. Amazingly, his father
had reconnected with Pierre Bourdon, whom he'd met before, at
an airport one day, while Rasquinet was still in his 20s. The father
had exchanged contact info with Pierre and subsequently handed the
perfumer's business card to Rasquinet.

This initiated a series of phone discussions and in-person dinners
between the retiring master and a suddenly-eager pupil-wannabe.
Eventually, Pierre decided Rasquinet had what it took – intellectually,
spiritually – to become his final student (after schooling Herault, Pierre
had begun to train Julie Masse, so put together, those three were the
final trio, with Rasquinet the least likely to have been picked and the
one who wound up seeming most like a son to Pierre and Kathy).

Olivier Creed did not know or care that Rasquinet was like family
to Pierre – merely that he had no diploma in the fragrance field
and needed assignments to make his mark and prove his worth to
a multinational (such as IFF, which would eventually hire Rasquinet,
in 2014, as it did Herault in 2010).

In fact, once Pierre finished schooling him, years before IFF took
notice of his work, Rasquinet moved to Dubai to work on the oud-
heavy briefs that market was generating in tremendous numbers.

Rasquinet has called it "a great idea laboratory, a place of intuition,
of excess."[60] (You can tell from his language alone why Proust-apostle
Pierre appreciated this humble and hirsute accidental poet Rasquinet.)
But above all, Dubai was the rare spot on the globe in need of perfumers.
His was an economically-motivated migration.

And so one can see why Olivier approached Rasquinet to ghostwrite

Creed scents – and why Pierre felt it improper yet again to deter a student from working with the tailor-weasel: Rasquinet needed the work, and sooner rather than later – he was 30 going on 31 when Olivier first approached him.

But the reason we speak of Rasquinet isn't just because he said yes to Olivier's pathetic, ignoble entreaties – thus making Rasquinet the actual author of Creed Royal Oud (2011) and Fleurs de Gardenia (2012) and also the entire "Acqua Original" line (2014), including the bizarrely-misspelled Aberdeen *Lavander*, Vetiver Geranium, Iris Tuberose, Asian Green Tea and Cedre Blanc and – no joke – the Creed children's cologne, Creed pour Enfants (2015).

It's because Rasquinet refused to speak to me for this project, in a way that makes Herault's sudden disappearance, the craven quality of his ghosting, understandable, inoffensive, sad.

Here's the message Rasquinet sent me on Instagram to decline my appeal.

"Thank you for your requests. I am sorry that I cannot answer your interview. I have the inexplicable hunch that it is better for me not to. I'm sure I'm wrong, so I apologize, but I won't change my mind. You will have noticed that one of the many faults of perfumers may be their stubbornness! If you have succeeded in interviewing several dozen perfumers, I think you will have a lot of material and I look forward to reading you."

Always well-spoken, Rasquinet unravels the recent history of Olivier Creed right here, including Herault's fearful retreat. How a non-perfumer such as Olivier ever attained the power and influence he did is itself a mystery, yet for these younger perfumers whom Pierre raised, it was a reality from day one.

It would be weirder if they weren't worried about what their honest discourse with me might do to jeopardize their lives and careers.

In fact, it's not just the power Olivier had already accumulated by the time Herault and Rasquinet rose to prominence that scares them – it his latter-day delusions. In dealing directly with Pierre, Olivier could never pretend with any commitment that he was the perfumer he claimed to be. That his words to the public would be lies was an accepted and discussed fact.

But with Pierre retired – and more on his moves upon leaving this bizarre world, momentarily – Olivier no longer felt entirely compelled to admit his professional shortcoming. He was more than double the age of Herault and Rasquinet.

Who were these neophytes to call bullshit to his face regarding his claim of being a perfumer?

(Although in private, Rasquinet has indeed said the entire Creed venture is a "sham," that Olivier "is incapable of constructing a perfume on his own" – but also that Olivier possesses "a great talent for evaluation" – and that sometimes, "he is also at the origin of the idea.")

While Rasquinet did not cooperate with me in the writing of this book, I nevertheless came across a story involving him that speaks to Olivier's scarily deluded state by the time of Pierre's retirement – his insistence even behind the scenes that he was a perfumer once Pierre was no longer in the picture.

This is a fuller version of a story told earlier in these pages:

Sometimes Olivier would come by Rasquinet's office and hand him a blotter strip – those thin paper arrows – resembling oversize collar stays – on which fragrance is sprayed for sampling, called a *mouillette* in French. Olivier would say, 'Have you smelt my most recent idea?'

Once, Rasquinet brought the paper to his nose, its odor both bewildering and amusing.

"Are you kidding me?" Rasquinet said to Olivier. "This is what I gave you last week!"

"He sincerely believed he had created the idea," Rasquinet tells associates when sharing this truly bizarre tale of Olivier's more recent magical thinking.

Which brings us back to the story of Herault – the man whose courage to discuss his involvement in the Creed perfume saga – the way he built the best masculine of this century within the framework of Pierre's technical principles but for Pierre's exploiter, Olivier – was short-lived.

I harbor no ill-will that our exchange ended after just a single deep-dive chat. But even were I inclined to, that resentment would be surpassed anyway by a great sympathy for Herault, for all the perfumers in Pierre's gloriously ragtag bunch (Kathy, Pierre's Roure-trained wife and occasional amanuensis, included):

These hustling souls of impressive erudition created a body of work unrivaled in its originality, influence and enchantment over the last 50 years.

And there's no greater proof of that than the massive proliferation of Creed clones– because Aventus wasn't the only formula unfairly co-opted by Creed that pirates then co-opted themselves.

Alongside the dupes of Creed Aventus, companies in the Middle East began issuing reverse-engineered-and-rebuilt versions of Green Irish Tweed and Silver Mountain Water and Millesime Imperial, too – all three of those being Pierre-created perfumes decades earlier pinched by Olivier.

Take Armaf, whose Dubai facilities provide a tremendous number of bottles to the Indian Subcontinent – but whose works somehow, via the web, wound up also penetrating the US. Armaf released Club de Nuit Intense Man (CDNIM) – an Aventus clone. But also Tres Nuit and Le Parfait, both Green Irish Tweed copies. Derby Club Blanche and Sillage – both Silver Mountain Water dupes. And Club de Nuit Milestone, a Millesime Imperial replica.

The same Amazon list that had CDNIM, the Aventus clone, ranked first in masculine EDP sales in 2021 also featured the Pierre dupes

Milestone at 16th and Sillage at 24th.

Amazingly, by pushing somewhat greedily for further scents by Pierre's students, Olivier Creed triggered an avalanche of replicas of his company's prior work. Creed's rapacity, while not remunerative for his decades-long ghostwriter, nevertheless had made Pierre a cross-cultural hero.

Do you know who knows the name of Pierre Bourdon? My friend – through the growing online fragrance community – Joy Amin, of Dhaka, Bangladesh, whose 60,000+ subscribers on YouTube are themselves learning more everyday about Kouros and Cool Water and Feminite du Bois. When they find out from this book that Pierre did the Creeds, too, they're gonna flip.

Yes, Olivier's past misdeeds are too massive to be redeemed by newfound, fair publicity for the actual artist.

But I like to imagine the dynamic thusly: Since Olivier's installation in a kind of fragrance industry throne was the result of his own agitprop, its debunking will force his metaphorical step-down – will thereby render his long reign in that chair mere seat-warming, a preparation for the rightful occupant to assume the spot. It will be Pierre's seat... because it always has been.

Romantic thinking, I know.

* * *

It's not entirely true that Jean-Christophe Herault and I got along perfectly well during our several hours of Zoom-chatting.

At one point, I raised the issue that Aventus fans most decry: the inconsistency of one batch to the next – the way one version smells fruitier than the bottles released just a month earlier, that some are smokier than others, that some seem to be pineapple bombs without much backing from the other ingredients, the well-roundedness of the redder batches, the ones with more noticeable apple, gone – a pineapple lopsidedness in its place.

As Jean-Christophe Herault formulated Aventus, one would think he'd know better than anyone whether batch variation was real instead of imagined on the part of Aventus fans, whether it was the result of quality control issues or formula modifications (either to save money or to comply with changing industry bans on certain materials due to their ability to trigger skin allergies over time).

But Herault gave the stock Creed answer, the one its devotees find least likely for very good reasons (to be relayed below): That the variation was entirely due to the high number of naturals in the formula, that their cultivation year-to-year gave them a slightly different smell, as terroir alters a wine depending on the weather across a growing season.

"Some year, the wine is super good, sometimes it's more fruity, sometimes it's more woody, sometimes, it's less good," Herault told me. But the key was what he said next: that the materials used to give the fragrance a smoky effect are especially sensitive to climate.

"If you have a different quality of this ingredient," he added, "it can change a little bit the perfume."

I nodded.

"But I know very well Olivier Creed," Herault told me. "This guy puts a lot of money in his perfume. It's not bullshit at all."

"No one would know more than you," I replied, no sarcasm intended at all.

Except that months later, I realized there was indeed a group of people who would know better than Herault – the scent pirates of Dubai whose gas chromatographic breakdowns of Aventus batches (enacted so they can build it back up but now as a clone – classic perfume reverse-engineering) had revealed that in fact different batches of Aventus actually did reflect slightly altered compositions.

Which doesn't mean Olivier spent less on any given batch – just that, behind the creator's back, Olivier had hired someone with the chemical competency to alter the formula, for whatever reason.

Could the scent-pirates have been lying to me? Perhaps. But that's what you learn quickly about the Dubai fragrance market. The pirates often know the work better even than its originator.

In this case, that would mean Olivier had, over the years, hired perfumers surreptitiously to tweak Herault's masterpiece without even letting the creator – let alone consumers – know.

Not a kind thing to do on many levels, though it wouldn't make Olivier the first fragrance *macher* guilty of such surreptitious switcheroos – in fact, the industry has a notorious history of messing with juices on the down-low.[61] Still, Olivier and Herault were no participants in a major, sterile corporate deal; theirs was a very intimate and personal relationship (or should have been based on the absolute lack of intermediaries).

"I'm sure Olivier respects his clients and the customers who buy Aventus," Herault said to me. "If there is anything different, it's because there are a lot of natural products in big amounts."

Not according to one of my sources, who says chemical breakdowns of various batches yield highly different results: Some have a greater pepper accord (materials whose sum effect is peppery, even if none by itself is), others more anise and blackcurrant, and still others with far less patchouli than Herault envisioned in his formula.

Unbeknownst to him – and completely behind his back, if his professed naivete/ignorance is to be believed – Herault's master formula was subject to constant tinkering – a treacherous and inartful interference artists in other fields would simply never abide.

(Although Herault perhaps should have realized all this sooner, ethics aside: by 2020, a newly-hired member of Creed's staff, one Chloe da Rocha, was already including in her LinkedIn profile her role in the "reformulation of perfume concentrates according to the different regulations.")

* * *

Maybe it shouldn't surprise anyone that Creed lacks a certain regard for his business associates and buyers when he's shown a deeper, though perhaps unintentional, disdain for his own ancestors. And here, I truly hope I am neither hurting his feelings nor inducing the sort of existential regret no measly fake-perfumer should ever have to feel. Truly.

There are two folders containing 300 pages in the National Archives of France dating from World War II on the relations between the Nazis overseeing Paris, a French collaborator with whom they worked named Henri A. Monnot des Angles, and the Creed tailoring shop on Rue Royale, then run by Henry Creed – Olivier's grandfather – and James Creed – Olivier's dad.

At the time, the women in the family – Olivier's aunts – were hunkered down for the war in a family home on St. Tropez called Villa Danielle.

Some of the pages are disturbing, if anticipated – the local collaborator is asked whether any Jews work for Creed. The Nazis decide that the Creeds are technically British, despite their having lived in Paris for 90 years. Henry Creed's salary must be held "in his favor" by some third party trustee at a local chapter of Barclays because Henry Creed's considered an enemy,[62] although not one dangerous enough to be arrested or prevented from tailoring tweeds.

Things get "Hogan's Heroes"-esque at points. The collaborator, Monsieur Monnot des Angles, must ask the Nazis whether the Bank of France, to which Henry Creed owes taxes, can take such excisions from his trustee account. Or, in basically his own words, if you won't let Creed collect his 10,000-Franc-per-month salary, but it's still being paid into a Barclays, you Nazis are gonna have to pay his taxes for him – which they did indeed end up doing.

(This is just the man's salary, of course; Henry Creed's equity in the company was a separate matter, dealt with on other forms, as were Mexican, Philadelphian and Yugoslavian bonds he held.)

But there is one instance in the files when Monnot des Angles actually resists the Nazis (just a bit):

"I would also like to draw your attention to the following fact," he writes to the Nazis in charge of Paris, in 1941. "The French Law of February 10, 1941, provides for exemptions on the restrictions on the sale of textiles in favor of Haute Couture Houses considered as creative industries. The Henry CREED house was proposed by the Chambre Syndicale de la Couture Parisienne to benefit from this exemption as a very old and very famous Maison de Tailleurs pour Dames."

That the Nazis rejected this request for laxity in the handling of the Creeds doesn't matter – it's all about the rationale the collaborator provided:

The Creed house is well known for its women's haute couture – to the point that even the couturiers' business association, its chamber of commerce, believes H. Creed should receive preferential treatment (and surely, the chamber did not recommend every such business be handled so lightly, or else its recommendations would be even more meaningless than they already were in the face of Third Reich obduracy).

In the end, it's no betrayal of his ancestors that Olivier shuttered an operation locals thought even Nazis might respect. But there's something very odd about what he did once that store did close:

He diminished – hid, really – the exact business activity his forebears hoped would provide them a measure of freedom in an occupied city.

He undermined the one claim the Creeds had under martial law to the unimpeded conducting of their historical work.

They were tailors. Famous for that trade alone. And damn good at it. Even a collaborating Frenchman challenged the Nazis to acknowledge as much.

I don't believe in karma, really, but there was no better time to review these 300 documents than the moment they arrived in my inbox – just days after my visit to the Dubai perfumeries who've made an industry out of selling Creed dupes, as if the IP were their own – as if the proprietor of the original company had abandoned *that* business.

Had, perhaps in retreat, claimed he'd never worked in the fragrance field at all.

Chapter 14: Revolution

On February 26, 2020, as a virus first noted in Wuhan was already spreading around the globe, about to press nearly all humanity into an unprecedented state of enforced immobility – adults and children alike freezing in place as if enacting a perversely grand variation of a playground game – American financial firm BlackRock announced that its Long-Term Private Capital fund, along with former Bacardi CEO Javier Ferrán, was acquiring Creed – in a private transaction, for an undisclosed amount.

Admittedly, I was at first surprised by this news – how had no one in the fragrance world hinted to me that this was forthcoming? Had I failed to cultivate truly helpful and generous sources?

I reached out to a bunch of my perfumer friends, who told me they were also caught unawares. But rather than comfort me, their reactions actually shocked me further – because they almost unanimously lamented the passing of yet another family fragrance enterprise, perhaps the final one to create all its scents in-house, per a multi-century tradition.

It was then I realized, to my horror, that even the worldliest of the present-day perfumers had bought into the *narischkeit* Creed narratives (some of which long preceded their entry into the industry, to be fair).

At that time, the book I was writing about the fragrance world was a far more expansive and varied volume than the one you've been reading. But it was perhaps this episode, in which the world's greatest perfumers exposed their own credulity, that first spurred me to consider taking on Creed in some major way, say by devoting to the fraudulent "family" enterprise an entire chapter.

I didn't know then that my own decision about a single section would lead a book agent to recommend I focus the entire initial foray into perfume on Creed's perfidy. Not that my dive into the subject will end here, with this account, or that this entire meta-discussion is here to explain my process.

It's actually to undermine the authority I've implicitly claimed in these pages – because if I was surprised by the BlackRock acquisition even months beyond its announcement, when it was finally and fully consummated, as I was, it's only because I wasn't properly paying attention in the first place.

First, behind the scenes, BlackRock created a British company, Fontaine Limited, through which it planned to control Creed *months* before a deal was ever announced – in December of 2019, or a quarter of a year before our lives as we knew them ended.

Second, the former US distributor and publicist of Creed, Laurice Rahme, told me how Olivier had kept pushing his son Erwin to spend time at raw materials firms and how much the young man had hated doing so – to the point that he actually decried his situation to her – confiding that his real passion, in a delicious plot twist, was to enter the fashion world – to become a high-end tailor!

"He was very unhappy," she told me.

Erwin had also spent time moonlighting as an occasional driver on the European racing circuit, an impressive feat, even if one only available to him in the first place because of his background (to that point, one of his three co-drivers in the 2018 edition of 24 Hours of

Le Mans was Romano Ricci, artistic director of tone-deaf perfumery "Juliette Has a Gun" but, more relevantly, the great-grandson of Nina Ricci, whose "L'Air du Temps" was the best-selling perfume in the US in the 1950s, taking in the same $30 million annually as Chanel No. 5; the third driver was the heir to Texan jewelry magnates).[63]

But at the very least, racing was an activity Erwin enjoyed. And his entry into storied races reflected not just a jet-setting lifestyle or a courage formed via upper class-coddling but a noble and spirited effort to make a name for himself (even if the logo of the Creed perfume brand adorned his car).

A perfumer with a range of connections seconded this story, essentially; he'd been told Erwin was fine with making money off the enterprise but wanted nothing to do with the actual fragrance work, found it a familial burden – just as his father had found tailoring and the creation of haute couture the very same.

Born in 1980, Erwin was fast-approaching an age at which Olivier himself had something of a midlife crisis, the age at which he began to distance himself from his actual heritage and fabricate an alternative: 40.

So Olivier must have feared, if he didn't sell the perfume business, it would not survive him – as his father's clothing operation hadn't lived on once Olivier took control (despite it having survived the Nazi occupation of Paris just decades earlier).[64]

But there was more to the sale beyond the company's ensured preservation that should've tipped me off to its near-term inevitability. Creed had gotten far too big — a result of Aventus, the sales of which also boosted the visibility of the company's other offerings – for a few not particularly distinguished businesspeople to run alone.

Olivier's choice as distributor of the Saujet brothers, whose warped idea of publicity led them to hand out perfume to maimed soldiers, was evidence enough that the expanded company required more accomplished professionals at the helm – needed to be a more a technocratic and meritocratic firm.

And so it has, in ways both obvious – the affiliation with the former Bacardi chief – and far less so – the major change at Creed's production site.

The latter subject was only touched on occasionally during those years when Olivier was appropriating Pierre's work left and right. And I couldn't tell you exactly when or to what degree Olivier took over the factory, but at some point while revving up production, Olivier (through a third party entity) gained control of a manufacturing site in the tiny village of Ury, a 3.2 square mile section of the Gatinais regional park with just 850 inhabitants whose demonyms are "Uriquois" and "Uriquoises."

Yes, Aventus, considered an all-time achievement in olfaction, was bottled by a small number of folks whose entire burg fits within a park (and perhaps this will ultimately become a hub, as another fragrance firm is set up nearby in the former production home of the Nina Ricci brand).

Just *how* bizarre is Ury as a source of Creeds?

The town features an Equestrian center but not a college or lycée. Its post office is open six days a week – but only from 9 am to noon. When the pandemic forced the community to postpone its nature festival till 2022, it hosted a discussion of snakes with a noted herpetologist entitled "Snakes: myths and reality," whose flyer copy read: "Have you ever seen a snake? Were you scared? What do you really know about them? Is a viper really dangerous?"

Ury hosts a "tree of the year" contest – Concours L'Arbre de L'Annee – which it promotes on Facebook with the exhortation: "You know a fantastic tree that deserves to be known, so enter…"

(Do I, though?)

Ury takes part in an animal monitoring effort called "Mission

Hedgehog," for which elected officials each morning search a tunnel located in a cemetery and covered in charcoal ink in the search for paw prints possibly left in the night.

As if in a film, the BlackRock acquisition has resulted in a descendance of city slickers on this sleepy country *ville*, at least in name if not in geographic reality (yet). And not just any city's slickers either, but London's, despite the US being Creed's biggest market.

BlackRock, having spoken to the Saujets, quickly moved to empower not those US distributor brothers but their infinitely more polished peers across the pond – the UK distributors of Creed, who called themselves The Orange Square Company.

It began on January 18, 2021, when the co-manager of the Ury factory resigned – a squat and imposing man, surname Gasche, whose shaved head recalled Mr. Clean but who'd treated me quite kindly in our correspondence and video chat.

Lean Monsieur Clean was replaced by Beatrice Ronfle Nadaud, who'd spent 10 years working in finance at Unilever and another 17 at AstraZeneca in various high-level financial positions.

This bespectacled, highly-numerate woman – her bouncy, bell-bottom-flared lob coif quite a contrast to her predecessor's chrome dome – was now the co- manager (along with a local) of the Creed factory – a job seemingly beneath someone of her experience and expertise.

But only three days later, BlackRock's plan became clear, when Ronfle Nadaud was named a director of the organization in London set up to run Creed – The Fontaine Group – and also that group's chief financial officer. Put more simply, she was appointed the CFO of Creed.

The now-apparent BlackRock strategy: to place its hand-picked experts not just in the c-suite but every facet of the firm's previously shady, bizarre, cut-rate operations.

In March, this new Fontaine entity bought the Orange Square Company – or, again, in non-corporate language: Creed purchased its UK distributor so as to hold an even firmer grip on all its operations.

And Ronfle Nadaud was not the lone newbie in control of the factory in Ury for very long, in fact. Three weeks later, she was joined by Sarah Jane Cook, CEO of Creed's UK distributor. They were then joined in June 2021 by Roberto Modica, a supply chain consultant who'd worked previously with fashion brands Loro Piana, Donna Karen and Façonnable.

BlackRock wasn't messing about – and with good reason. A small-time mentality had reigned previously inside Creed, because Olivier hadn't cared for actual business and those he empowered hadn't fully managed to compensate for that indifference (no matter their tall tales).

Yes, Creed had begun to rake in dough, but it still had a kind of ragtag, random quality to its work. And that started with the North American operation run by the Saujets, whose office on West 25th Street in the Flatiron district of Manhattan was literally a couple-minute stroll from my own NYC apartment. An amble I happily offered to make in advance of my writing a word about the perfumery or its American doofus-dons, so they could inspect me in the flesh.

By Feb. 4, 2020, before the BlackRock acquisition of Creed was announced, I was in email correspondence with the senior director of corporate communications for the US. From the jump, she told me I "likely" couldn't interview Erwin Creed either by phone or in person – Erwin is Olivier's son and the supposed seventh-generation perfumer in the patrilineal chain (I had asked to chat with him because I figured it far a more easily-fulfilled request than calling for the time and attention of his pops).

This predated any pandemic restrictions, but here's the best this publicist could do: "We could *look* into getting your questions answered over email" (the italics are my own) – but only if I could explain to her satisfaction who I was and what sort of book I intended to write.

I did, and not long after, she approved my entreaty, urging me to send her the questions for Erwin so she could begin work on getting them answered. She later wanted to send Erwin some of my old press clippings. And score for me an interview with Emmanuel Saujet.

I sent along my queries:

My very first question for Erwin involved the work of my grandfathers in the garment business – one ran a humble workwear firm that held the contract to create winter coats for the New York City Department of Sanitation; the other, after surviving the Holocaust and resettling in the Bronx, managed a zipper factory in Manhattan. Neither are figures I invoke lightly. I was opening up about my fashion patrimony so Erwin might feel comfortable doing the same.

But he never had the chance. The chief of staff for Creed North America, upon returning from a vacation I hadn't known she was on, immediately put the kibosh on the interview upon reentering the office – a full 20 days into my now-amicable dialogue with her colleague, weeks after I'd sent over the question list for Erwin.

Sign a contract with a publisher first, the chief of staff said, "and then we can revisit the request based on availability."

Even now I shake my head at that response – because I'd repeatedly offered to handle her operation with kid gloves, though I may have done so officiously and with some unfortunate reportorial hubris.

"I know the specs of Erwin's Audi RS6, and that Emmanuel Saujet lives not far…from Elvis' old house," I said. "If you're in the business of protecting the Creed brand, ensuring its stature while it grows, I'm the person you want nearby, as a friend of the company, not out in the open as an unloosed reporter researching all sorts of matters."

The chief of staff never took the hint – and neither did she respond a year later when I essentially reintroduced myself and tried to reset relations after I'd indeed found a publisher.

But BlackRock was a real-deal firm, and its hires for the new Creed corporate office in London – located just above the posh Ivy Soho Brasserie, with its red banquettes – demonstrated as much. The new chief marketing officer – Giles Gordon – had worked at Japanese fragrance firm Kao and at L'Oréal and had most recently served as marketing director for Dyson.

Giles himself reached out to me after less than three months on the job and couldn't have been kinder. He told me the new Creed execs were working on a book about the brand themselves, and so he had some questions about my own effort.

"It's not a coffee table book?" he asked, then querying me about the likely price. No, no, I assured him – I am not planning that sort of glossy, luxury offering (convinced as I said it that his book in development was indeed of that variety – not that such knowledge would ever affect my own mission).

The idea of competition dismissed, Giles even offered to collaborate, saying it might be useful for his team and me if they shared some of the Creed info a deep-dive nonfiction book required.

Sounded good – especially because he'd never asked what I thought of Olivier or even mentioned the issue of perfume authorship. Perhaps this kind chap knew painfully well the degree to which his predecessors had played loosely with the truth. Perhaps there were small ways in which this new cabinet was not only willing to cop to that dishonesty but help expose it, so that it could face the future more boldly, unbound by decades of oratory it would never be so dumb as to originate.

What if we really were in this struggle together – a correction of the past, a pursuit of truth in the present? I thought, after my chat with Giles. Hell, a properly-done Creed book could even celebrate the manifold talents of the real perfumers, Pierre included, though of course, I wanted to be the first to credit Bourdon so lavishly.

But that fear of being scooped soon metamorphosed. Three weeks after our Microsoft Teams talk, Giles nixed in rather sterile language our further working together. "We have decided this is something that we would not be able to contribute to," he wrote. "This is especially pertinent because, as I mentioned, we are working on a number of our *own* projects at this time."

Not only did this not sound like the dude I'd come to know a few weeks back – it seemed to indicate a desired separation on the part of Creed – as if the new c-suite, having spent just a bit more time on the job, realized my own enterprise would by necessity have to expose seediness they sought to paper over, quite literally.

Following the company's social media accounts, I began to worry, perhaps in a quintessentially writerly way, what all this new marketing copy might augur: A book that dismissed Olivier's duplicity as Kaufman-esque marketing stunt or benign imaginative art project – instead of a decades-long fraud.

I didn't want them, in beating me to a printing press, to undermine the seriousness of a story not-yet-told – to render my digging silly, to define the terms of what had occurred per their own objectives, such that my work might be dead-on-arrival, if writing can be said to have a life at all (and I really pray it can).

Was I crazy to harbor such ideas, a wannabe-perfume-poet turned paranoiac?

Well, there *was* precedence for this sort of race to define the legacy and culture of a vaunted fragrance firm and its namesake. In 1985, Random House and Macmillan, aware of each other's plans, competed to publish first a book on Estee Lauder and her billion-dollar business – the former ostensibly written by its subject, meant to be a memoir *and* a guide to hosting parties (no, really), the latter an investigative look by Lee Israel, who later forged letters ostensibly penned by famous literary figures and was played by Melissa McCarthy in a film called

"Can You Ever Forgive Me?"

The idea behind Lauder's own work was to defuse whatever bombs Israel might plan on dropping. Thusly, she copped for the first time to being born in Queens and not some enchanted European principality, though she declined to elaborate on the romantic affair with the future head of IFF Israel unveiled.

Yes, it had been long ago and the book world had become considerably less combative since, but the power of the press, though diminished, hadn't similarly depreciated the power of precedence (which the always-on Internet and its social media might have even increased).

And given the audacity of past Creed copy, who was to say what maneuvers legit execs might undertake to legitimize the venture – what disclosures might be penned to decrease the effect of my own – a venture whose acquisition cost its new owners nearly $1 billion?

They were in a tough spot.

And I felt myself increasingly squeezed into one, too, as my would-be buddy Giles posted an 8-second clip of a big and thick and glossy publication rolling along the conveyor belt of a printing press, alongside this cryptic message:

So excited for this secret Creed brand project now coming to life. Huge thanks and congratulations to everyone involved, you know who you are. It is just the beginning! #brand #marketing #luxury #storytellers.

That the cover bore the name "Creed" in large, unmistakable letters only made the admittedly beautiful object's divining more difficult:

Was this the coffee table book of which Giles had spoken? And yet, it seemed from that banner atop the cover to be formatted like a periodical. Was Creed launching a lifestyle magazine besides the aforementioned monograph?

I suddenly began imagining the business opportunities – the Creed name, were it to become synonymous with a certain lifestyle, could very well be licensed for the name of a luxury hotel. Or several.

I only had two real journalistic tasks remaining in order to complete this section of my larger perfumer-focused work. Travel to Dubai, to dive into its manifold copies of Pierre's perfumes and Herault's, too. To see for myself the extent of the fragrance pirating that made those two the most famous unknown craftsmen in the world.

And then to travel to France itself, first to Paris, where so many of my sources and contacts and friends were finally able to go out for dinner after months of curfew and then to Normandy – to visit the rustic estate of Pierre Bourdon himself, to talk with him and Kathy in person, finally.

Always, I'd planned on these meetings because nothing could alter their import: A story of a genius and his perilously-suave manipulator always had to end with my meeting the former, otherwise I'd be myself complicit in the diminishment I shame.

A burbling brook surrounds Pierre's land two hours north of Paris – although I don't know the precise term for this crooked little stream. But having eyed it before I'd ever met Pierre, I saw it as a kind of topographic talking-to, an admonition from the earth:

It's from this source here that all these creations – scrambled and confused for the public by a bizarre roster of the corrupt and the cowardly – emerged. And it's to the very same wellspring any telling of the Creed story must, in the end, return.

If I made enemies of the new owners, so be it. The time had come for me to visit Pierre and Kathy – for us to commune in person with a camaraderie we all seemed already to feel.

I didn't know whether I'd beat Creed to the punch. I just knew Pierre's life warranted that effort.

France opened its borders to traveling Americans for the first time in many months on June 9, 2021.

My flight was June 10.

Chapter 15: Du côté de chez Bourdon, or, Pierre's Way

June 2021.

I stay in the 48-room Hotel Mistral, on Rue Cels, in the 14th Arrondissement – residence of Simone de Beauvoir and Paul Sartre from 1937-1939 and "then on various occasions during the war," according to the plaque posted just outside the entrance.[65] That my fellow guests and I pass this sign, with its light-handed treatment of Europe's darkest and most destructive hour, wearing masks, only our eyes and foreheads visible, should perhaps give me more pause than it does.

But I am focused on the meeting that has been a year and a half in the making – what I consider to be the great culmination of all my research so far. Which means, having paid a visit a couple days earlier to Proust's resting spot in the Pere Lachaise – his black slab monument low to the ground and horizontal, the impassive ebony of a dilated pupil – I don't even bother venturing to the Cemetery of Montparnasse just a block east of my hotel, home of the Cenotaph of Baudelaire and the graves of Guy de Maupassant and Serge Gainsbourg.

The night before and early that morning I run all the necessary pre-trip errands, traipsing up and down Rue Daguerre, the bustling little shop-filled thoroughfare made famous in the 1976 documentary

"Daguerréotypes" by Agnes Varda, a resident of the block from 1950 till her death in 2019 (call me a softy, but later, watching a news clip in which a woman in sunglasses says, *"La rue Daguerre me fera toujours penser à Agnès Varda,"* I can't help but cry).

I pick up gluten-free boule from Le Comptoir de Milana and several bottles of water for the two-hour drive to the Château de la Vicomté – the nearly-200-year-old castle-home of Pierre and Kathy Bourdon. And I purchase madeleines and scotch as gifts for the hosts.

I'm anxious to leave as 8 am slips quickly toward 9, but Shyam – Shyamala Maisondieu, the Givaudan perfumer accompanying me on this sortie – wants to have her coffee and breathe for a moment, and as she's driving, she's well within her right, sorta (and yet, what if we're tardy and we're turned away from Chez Bourdon altogether, deemed insolent and inconsiderate? What if a moment's sipping makes all the difference?).

I take in my caffeine with a peevish aspect at a table outside the beautiful bistro Augustin.

* * *

Another take entirely.

Olivier Creed, after everything he'd done, no more a villain than perhaps a dozen other folks in the perfume industry, he could be redeemed – *partially* – perhaps not on personal merit but on the demerits of the industry entire.

It's all relative. And perfumery isn't the domain of a single Svengali – it's rife with compromised characters carrying out schemes of questionable ethics.

There are clones whose outrageous pricing makes an implicit claim for originality. Several scents from the very expensive and supposedly-Italian brand Xerjoff are widely-viewed as dupes of

Chanels – Richwood as Coromandel, Oden as Allure Homme Blanche.

Of course, Coco Chanel herself was a Nazi spy – Abwehr Agent F-7124 – whose code name was "Westminster" and who was tasked with the further recruitment across Europe of potential Third Reich spooks.

YSL's Opium simply mimicked Estee Lauder's Youth-Dew, a scent created for Estee by the lover she took during a three-year separation from her husband Joe (whose surname was "Lauter" until they got back together and he inserted the "D" – a move into which a Freudian might read much).[66]

There's the former Guerlain marketer Roja Dove, whose brazenly borrowed output is impossible to exculpate, even if he was kind and open with me (he enjoys watching "Schitt's Creek"; he told me that the hardest moment of his life was the passing of his mother).

His Roja Parfums' Danger takes after Heritage de Guerlain. Diaghilev mimics Mitsouko. Fetish is highly reminiscent of Hermes Bel Ami. Enslaved smells like Molinard Habanita. Oligarch recalls wearers of Terre d'Hermes.

(And while we're on the subject of high-end copying, why did Tom Ford, a man of endless creativity it appears, okay Tom Ford Noir of 2013, an obvious clone of Guerlain Habit Rouge? Why was he cool with Beau du Jour being a very slightly-altered Zino Davidoff of 1986? And recall the former US distributor of Creed – Laurice Rahme – if she was so morally superior to Olivier, why was the signature men's scent of her new brand, Chez Bond, seemingly a hybrid of Pierre Bourdon's Green Irish Tweed and Cool Water? And don't get me wrong – I love Tom Ford's stuff, and Laurice has treated me so kindly.)

And as for Roja's identity as a fragrance-formulator, which he assumed after his late-career departure from Guerlain (whose scents seemingly inspired his own, as mentioned above), it's playacting of superlative chutzpah — by nearly all accounts public and private.

A 1994 Daily Mail article referred to Roja as a "make-up artist."[67] The Irish Times, 1997: Roja is a makeup application teacher.[68] The Herald (of Glasgow) in 1998: Roja is "essentially a perfume teacher."[69]

Sylvaine Delacourte, former artistic director of Guerlain, in an email to me: "Roja Dove was my student and did not study perfumery! *Beaucoup* of lies in the industry!"

And yet, by the account of one perfumery insider, since launching his eponymous brand, Roja has threatened to sue anyone who asserts he isn't the formulator of the products that bear his name.

Then there are the double identities – perfumer Chris Maurice is also perfumer Christian Carbonnel, for instance.

And triples identities with a touch of criminality: Pierre Montale, the putative perfumer of Montale and Mancera fragrances, previously known as Pierre Durrani, is originally Pierre-Louis Repellin,[70] a co-owner of the well-known fragrance brand Comptoir Sud Pacifique for a quarter-century – a man once featured in a French Vogue society snapshot – who was nevertheless sued in the 1990s for counterfeiting a Jean-Paul Gaultier fragrance after copying its bottle and making his work seem that of JPG's at a glance.[71]

(The initiation of this case was highly cinematic. The authorities descended upon not just Repellin's venture but all stores and companies doing business with him – i.e. those producing the forgery and those retailers vending it, including: a Monoprix store and Monoprix's head office; the head office of Galeries Lafayette; the office of the companies Parfums Concept and Durrani Parfums Concept in Cannes; the Office Maritime Monégasque; and the Thermoforage company.)

In fact, this court finding, that Pierre Montale conspired to rip off the consumer, may very well have been the impetus for his cofounding the new brand with Atmeh:

The appeals court imposed a helluva lot of fees and fines Pierre-Louis Repellin couldn't escape paying – nearly a billion Francs total, or about $143,000 (a sliver of which was to be born not by Repellin but the supermarkets that retailed his knockoff, as the entire arrangement from beginning to end was impudent mimicry; the bottle's design *and* marketing made it seem a Gaultier, and the court documents described the operation as "parasitism").

Owing the parent company of Gaultier that hefty sum, then, Repellin co-founded the Montale brand – which is not an eponym but a a marque inspired by retired Italian footballer Vincenzo Montella (these two wiseguys felt an Italian-sounding name would impart to their startup a measure of prestige).

And then, betrayal.

The other Montale cofounder, Ammer Atmeh,[72] told me Pierre took cover behind some rather intimidating Gulf businessmen and essentially pushed him out of the company from that protected position, though Atmeh did receive a $2 million settlement (which he claims was presented to him after a visit from a hired Algerian thug and another street fighter-type and which he signed only because he was under duress).

I'm not saying Atmeh is a totally blameless boy scout, by the way; he strikes me as the sort of person who would bend the truth if it meant taking in more dollars or dirhams (you don't just become partners with someone as obviously immoral as Repellin). For what it's worth, at one point during the pandemic, Atmeh had given up selling perfume for a period to try and make money vending personal protective equipment. This was during a major shortage – I've been curious ever since how he sourced the material.

Meanwhile, back when they were business partners and bosom buddies, Repellin and Atmeh even went to Disneyland together. Then Repellin disappeared with a cache of Montale bottles and ghosted Atmeh – who, after finally tracking him down via private investigator, had to spend five years in court trying to recapture his own company from Repellin.

This hasn't stopped a single department store from retailing Montale. Fan-favorite Montale Intense Café – in August 2021 – goes for $170 at Bloomingdale's. Neiman Marcus charges the same price for Montale Roses Musk.

An incredible case of sniff-no-evil (but stay tuned to hear me cop to the same sin).

That Repellin, who almost never grants requests for interviews, now calls himself by the name of his ostensibly-stolen and definitely-murky business – you must address him as "Pierre Montale" – just adds a whole level of weirdness absent from the Creed story. The tailor of our tale never renamed himself after the juices Bourdon provided him. Or later insist on the *nom* "Olivier Aventus."

In fact, even some of Olivier's Aventus claims seem not so wild when contextualized.

He claimed ridiculously that Aventus was inspired by the life of Napoleon Bonaparte, but he wasn't really alone in sharing with one and all such a grandiose link. A century earlier, legendary perfumer Francois Coty pulled a similar stunt, though his surname was actually "Spoturno," and already, one wondered whether Coty wasn't part phony: Creed-like, Coty made to sure claim in the press constantly, while using this invented moniker, that he was most definitely a Corsican descended from Bonaparte.

"In Paris, where he lives, little that is precise is known about him even when he says it himself," wrote The New Yorker of Coty in 1930.[73]

Uncannily contemporary, this line. Can one merely say, then, Olivier Creed came down with what Coty had 100 years ago – guilty of a Katz's deli, I'll have what she's having-type immorality? Are sins much reduced when they're not new under the sun – perhaps not really singular at all? (Turn, turn, turn.)

Oh, and Francois Coty was no less enamored of the glistering luxury on Rue Royale than Olivier – Coty wanted a piece of that highlife, in the same way Olivier must've when his old neighbor on the block, Maxim's, was the site of the blowout launch party for YSL Kouros (a Bourdon creation).

And so Francois Coty, 100 years ago, became the first perfumer ever to walk into Lalique and strike a deal to sell his scents in that firm's glassware.

And then there's pure Pierre, our beloved Bourdon, whose every rejection nudged him that much closer to a retirement early by perfumer standards (or, early by the standards of male stars – the women of commensurate talent and experience seem to get pushed into jobs outside the competitive briefing world much younger; they're asked to take up new posts running training programs; from what little I've seen, they're made to feel used up – and yes, the men will be, too, in time, but their departures seem far more kindly choreographed).

So Pierre handed over to Olivier these rejected formulas with a brooding melancholy – an indifference born of an unfortunate tendency Pierre has to imagine each loss connected to the prior one – to experience life's disappointments as parts of a single larger episode, as mounting one atop the other, like a snowstorm that, falling not long after a similarly strong blizzard a day before, cascades not onto the city's concrete and grass but onto the white layer already blanketing those surfaces – and every other.

Pierre in the face of unfair putdowns: *This is just more snow on snow on snow* (#BachsOnBachsOnBachs).

But a perfumer does not have to respond to failure this way at all. Olivier Gillotin at Givaudan, after losing a brief, will study the scent that beat him out and then produce as many copies of that winning formula for *other brands* as possible.

He doesn't get down – he gets even. And he ain't the lone nose in the aroma arena to bear a grudge.

So who's really to blame if Pierre doesn't have inside that industry-necessitated junkyard dog in him? Is it not a trade that deals in the evanescent, whose every characteristic tells you upfront, You can be bounced whenever? Did his pops exhaust Pierre's ability to protect himself?

Where's the resilience?

Oh, and a small twist: I own and wear an Italian clone of Pierre's YSL Kouros called "Arrogance," along with the original. I happily own also a bottle of a leathery Montale fragrance (although this one was released in 2006, before Repellin and Atmeh fell out) and innumerable decants from various batches of Creed Aventus. And from a handful of Rojas.

Am I separating the art from the artist with thoughtfulness and sophistication or am I just full of it?

This was the other side. Another take entirely.

There is a Japanese proverb at least a couple centuries old worth repurposing here perhaps. Of the mediocre figure, someone who neither helps nor harms others, a nonentity, it can be said, rather rhythmically: *"Jinkou mo takazu he mo hirazu"* – this person neither burns oud nor passes gas.

A great little saying on a number of levels, but one whose application seems far too narrow. Rather than pick on a middling person, let us use it instead to describe everyone – in this book, in life – because there's no soul who's ever engaged entirely in just one of these activities. We all try to perfume ourselves with whatever we believe will enhance us (perhaps that's not an olfactive adornment but an Instagram filter – either way). And yet we are all in the end subject to weaknesses and faults that can't be airbrushed, scented, suppressed.

Creed may claim as its slogan *"De pere en fils depuis 1760."* How much more beautiful I'd find its work – how many sins I'd so readily forgive on behalf of others – if just once, for one run of bottles, they replaced that meaningless, elitist, fictional phrase with the above...

Jinkou mo takazu he mo hirazu.

Olivier Creed inhales a chai latte at the Starbucks at 67th and Columbus, Jan. 22, 1999, so a Times writer can record the Frenchman's take: "Too much cinnamon." (Courtesy of Chang W. Lee/The New York Times/Redux)

So many ghosts occupy Rue Royale yet – perhaps some – having known well his father and uncle – are waiting for Olivier to realize finally his haberdasher life was no embarrassment, he was quite blessedly cut from the same cloth as his predecessors (pun intended) and could've made a splendid – even debauched and diverting – career out of the clothing trade – and that he's welcome yet to return to his block – to come home and work beneath its quaint and lasting stone signage.

Lalique remembers what the street once was. And would a snobby waiter at an institution such as Maxim's even have realized Olivier had been gone for a few decades?

Of course, as I pursued that story of identity, fear, prodigal escape, Olivier was secretly already planning on cutting ties with his fraudulent fragrance dynasty, though seemingly not to purge his soul but stuff his pockets. Perhaps in so doing he was losing the chance to take a load off – because whatever moolah he could get from a deal might add to the weight he already felt pressing upon him.

A man who faked his way through life had a chance to repent publicly. But the window in which to try was getting smaller by the day. Olivier Creed had already brought in the top investment bankers, including one French group particularly expert at selling small prestigious lux brands to the beauty world's biggest conglomerates.

* * *

Shyam and I finish our espresso and she hustles to pick up her claret-colored Mini Cooper Clubman (the vehicle supplied her by Givaudan, so valuable is she as a perfumer). I'm waiting on the side of the road, by the cemetery. I'm already sweating – it's my last day in France, and I've burned through all my packed outfits already – except for a nice pair of chinos unsullied by me but the unfortunate victim of a wooden chair whose red paint clung to my ass cheeks when I stood up.

So I'm wearing stonewashed jeans with a hole at the left knee and a chunky, loosely-knit Hilfiger wool sweater only half-buttoned up (for the purpose of aeration, but also, yes, to affect that hirsute Burt Reynolds look that evokes Playgirl spreads and "Boogie Nights" – and also actual *boogie nights*). I've sprayed myself, too, with Kouros Fraicheur, the slightly lighter (but still highly sex-panthery) 1993 version of Kouros Pierre authored for Saint Laurent.

One minute becomes five becomes 10, the early morning cloud cover dissipating, the sun beating its way through the dun, pendulous clouds

– hot beams now drawing out long beads of sweat from my forehead, from between my shoulder blades. I wanna tell her, What the hell – why couldn't we have picked up coffee on the way and wasn't your car just around the corner to begin with? Ten minutes seems soon to be 20.

But besides loving Shyam, there's another reason I won't carp too much about her driving – or I'll kinda try not to, at least – which will soon turn out to be wilder than Annie Hall's, as disturbing as Duane's, the stop-starting of her petite feet against the pedals, herky-jerky and nauseating, drawing from me long sighs followed by small moments of near-whispered importuning – *Just a little smoother here, a little more assertive switching lanes there, please. Accelerate! Pretty please!*

Ultimately, I realize whatever I say will be heard for the truth it's barely concealing – that this ride is sickening – and so by the return trip, I've channeled all my complaints into lectures on the *general* benefits of driving mocs and how she'd really benefit greatly from a change in footwear, proceeding to do my best Mars Blackmon interpretation for the Malaysian beauty unlikely to have ever even once heard that Spike Lee *nom de cine*.

"Money, it's gotta be the shoes."

But, as I said, there's another reason for me to curb the snide commentary (not that I succeed) – and it's that Shyam's no random perfumer in relation to the two-hour drive into Normandy, to the meeting of Pierre at his remote home – with its rectangular pool surrounded by sculptures and then a wilder, non-rectilinear yard, marked by a dirt path through shaded trees, all of it surrounded by a *tashlich*-appropriate brook.

Pierre spent a decade at a Japanese fragrance company – Takasago – the highest executives of which, not caring for strong scent per Japanese tradition, had no enthusiasm for the artistry and craft of perfumery in the first. Shyam, having spent years at Kao, also a

Japanese beauty company, will surely be able to relate in ways I cannot.

Then, more significantly, there's the broken path that led me to Paris, only days earlier, as soon as the country opened its borders again to Americans and the compulsory curfew for residents, having begun at 5 pm and then progressed during the reopening stages to 7 and then 9, finally reached 11 pm.

Any *one* story about how I got into a perfumery would be a lie – there are a multiplicity of reasons, and it feels almost random which I share when asked. But here's one for real: the only reason I ever got an internship in Esquire's fashion department (from which, at the end of the summer, I wound up stealing a bottle of Jean-Paul Gaultier Le Male and Jacques Cavallier's Rive Gauche pour Homme Light) is because I pressed editor Nick Sullivan for one at an Esquire sponsored-event in Macy's in Herald Square in the spring of 2005.

That I attended the event in the first place speaks to how tired and silly and egotistical I must have then been in my senior year of high school: Esquire was holding a contest to find the best-dressed man in America, and I decided to enter, as if that made any sense.

I wore a blue oxford shirt and a tie fashioned originally from a yellow, paisley-ornamented bandanna (I think) but wound up utterly overwhelmed by the 88 other brave souls, some of whom drove from out of state, including one from Delaware and another from Baltimore (the winner, then 32, hailed from Yonkers).

Who judged us? You might be wondering. Well, ad man Donny Deutsch, whose TV gig on CNBC hadn't been cancelled yet, and Allan Houston, the beloved shooting guard who'd just retired from the Knicks. They sat on a dais, believe it or not, as all of us contestants strutted down a runway, one after the other.

But that was only half the shindig. Because the party doubled as a fragrance release event for Armani's new men's scent Black Code (whose name would be changed simply to "Code" only months later when Armani's license-holder, L'Oréal, found out the term hard some racist meaning among white supremacist groups).

And after the runway portion had ended, we all just mingled on Macy's men's floor, as servers passed around bottles of Black Code and also drinks.

The kicker is that Black Code was made for L'Oréal by Shyam's then-husband Antoine – she knew every little thing about that scent as it was constructed. The bigger kicker: the Esquire style editor I accosted to score an internship, wore as his signature scent Green Irish Tweed – i.e. the first of Pierre Bourdon's secretly ghostwritten blockbuster successes for Olivier. A Pierre classic.

I had no idea at that Macy's party that the scents I encountered that night would later form the bookends – karmic boundaries – of a trip deep into the soul of the perfume industry. But now, in the plague summer of 2021, such connections were too weird to ignore, too exciting not to push to the limit.

So Shyam, an expert on Armani Code, drove me however erratically deep into the country – to see the man who devised my style section editor's scent. I knew about the ghost before I ever knew about him. I began to write about perfumery before he ever acceded to my visiting him.

Life is amazing.

* * *

Olivier didn't just bring in any investment bank or consultancy as Aventus generated incredible revenues and his son showed far more enthusiasm for racing around Le Mans than pretending to be a perfumer. No, Olivier brought in advisers whose entire raison d'être is to get founder-led beauty firms into the hands of the few mammoth grooming groups:

Michel Dyens & Co.

When By Kilian, which had created some of my favorite scents as an indie brand (even if one run by an heir to the Hennessey liquor fortune), sold itself in 2016 to Estee Lauder, it was advised by Dyens. One year earlier, when Korean skincare firm Have & Be sold itself to Lauder, it was advised by Dyens. A year prior to that, when salon products-maker Colomer was sold to Revlon, it was advised by Dyens.

Note the lack of variability in the M&A destinations here – it's to make me think maybe the FTC should give the sector a look.

But no matter the legality of that concentrated power, the fact was, and remains, that Michel Dyens is the firm you call when you're ready to quit – that is, when the money generated by your trendy-but-not-yet-truly-widespread beauty biz or frag firm is so good you'd be a fool to resist. But also, a *tired* fool – because you've spent years building up this venture – how much further can you reasonably take it before you collapse underneath the weight and pressure?

Olivier wasn't actually formulating his scents but that doesn't mean the publicity their sale required was also an illusion. Olivier had been traveling the world for four decades by 2020 to tout the quality of Creed concoctions (no matter his invented role in their creation).

Nobody can push products for decades without growing weary, and Olivier's face revealed he was no exception: The handsome man was still that, but that veiny tired skin under his eyes attested to the rigors of a nonstop roadshow. Olivier wasn't the hardest worker – his old US distributor made him sound lazy as hell to me. But perhaps a large portion of his exhaustion was the physical toll exacted by the ceaseless fabrication, by his need to be on-guard, vigilant not to disclose any truth after having christened some new Creed boutique in the UAE or Far East or even New York.

Travel is all well and good until you have to remember not just where you are but whom in that moment you're supposed to be.

Which is to say, as soon as Olivier picked up the phone to dial Dyens & Co., the decision had been made, even if no words had passed between company head and consultancy. Even if Olivier himself thought he was just edging his toe into the pool, simply taking the temperature of the water.

When the sale was announced, the new Creed company made sure to emphasize that Olivier would have a continued role at the firm. And yet it was hard not to see him as a mere figurehead now – beyond a mere stand-in for a ghostwriter – just a kind of cardboard cutout of a man.

Here he is sniffing flowers by a coastline – let's post this on Instagram and keep up the idea of the man's non-stop nosework. Who cares that he is wearing a white golf polo made by FootJoy but no other sports gear – that he seems prepared neither for perfume formulation nor golf, just for standing there, a blank look on his face, as if such were his sinecurist role – posing – like a broken-down, near-senescent Joe Louis standing outside Caesar's Palace as a "greeter" in 1970, his days as America's great superhero, vanquisher of Nazis in the public mind, long gone – taken for granted or simply forgotten.

Time is equally unkind to the skilled and those who have pretended to be.

But BlackRock did brilliantly in hiring for Creed a new CEO. Her name was Sarah Rotheram, and while perhaps her greatest asset to the company was her prior work experience as CEO of British perfumeries Miller Harris and Penhaligon's (technically, the parent company of Penhaligon's but close enough), her entire attitude since she was 14 made her the right candidate for the renewal a morally-bankrupt Creed required.

See, she'd spent her whole life since that age – when she interned for an interior designer in a cottage in Essex – eyeing old pieces of furniture with great beauty but also issues, all born of usage or simply the unstoppable passing of time (nicks, rips, worn upholstery) and reviving them – sometimes even making them appear more contemporary and modern than their maker ever could have dreamed decades earlier upon their release.

She wasn't just a collector of antiques nor was she was someone drawn to the old simply due to that age. She was an imaginative projector – someone who could see the bones of a piece and visualize how great it could be once those basic elements were rebuilt-upon – properly re-ornamented with paint or fabric or cushioning.

No matter that Pierre had built the structure now in question instead of Olivier, Creed indubitably possessed similarly tremendous bones – a catalog of fragrances created by a true master and his two students – a product whose obsessive clientele shells out hundreds per bottle (and that's not including the rare batches sold on eBay for up to $50,000 for 4 oz.).

An accomplished perfume executive with longstanding love of – and expertise at – salvaging structurally brilliant items? Who better to take the Creed reins?

(She's also a major reader and a collector of funky sneakers, a further two qualities I rate highly.)

I thought this even as her office, particularly the chief marketing officer working alongside her, suddenly froze me out after confiding in me Creed was preparing its own book.

In a way, no one is a bigger fan than I – because I know the fate of Pierre's genius work actually lies in Sarah Rotheram's hands. My only questions were: Does she know truly who made these items within her grasp?

And if so, would she ever be able or allowed to tell that truth – would Creed somehow, starting in 2021, begin to acknowledge the genius behind its work?

I wanted the answer to be yes, but I also wanted to get out my own work first, before Creed – the company, not the decaying man – finally copped to this amazing – and no less novelistic than the tomes Rotheram reads while traveling – legacy of co-opting.

* * *

Shyam and I take the A13 north, in the direction of Rouen (site of Monet's purplish cathedral paintings), later crossing the Risle, the 90-mile-long river in Normandy that, flowing south to north, in the same direction of our vehicle, as it were, ends up as a tributary of the Seine.

Pierre's more specific directions were hilariously provincial (especially as they came from a man who'd scented millions the world over): "After 1.9km you will see on your left a large black garbage can and a dead end sign..."

We end up heading down a narrow and curved driveway to the chateau – one that seems a squeeze even for Shyam's Mini. And yet we have made it, and Pierre and Kathy are right outside to grab what bags we have (mine consists of liquor and madeleines).

Kathy is wearing a white sleeveless dress with a chunky necklace of different-colored seemingly-glass spheres and translucent earrings of the same material and shape, rectangular tortoise-shell spectacles, her hair up in a bun. Three golden bracelets dangle from her right wrist.

She is immediately welcoming – which isn't to say Pierre isn't, only that she's clearly the one in this pair who makes the pronouncements. Who marks appearance of the guests aristocratic-party style — *Announcing the Count and Countess of Creed-focused Copy, Hobo-Chic Gabe and Shyam of Malaysia.*

Pierre, not trailing far behind his other half, even if their difference in volume seems to indicate otherwise, strikes me as more handsome and virile – less bookish-looking – than I'd assumed he would from photos.

He's bedecked in summer wear – a gingham button-down shirt of sea-green stripes; slim chinos of a similar color (perhaps these are closer to lime or mint); and dark loafers, worn properly preppy *sans* socks. His left pinky boasts a stone ring and his embroidered belt features multi-colored arrows and rectangles that my non-sailing self assumes are nautical flags. His left wrist features a watch that even from a decent distance seems of considerable value.

His glowing skin bespeaks his routine of swimming each day in his stately pool and then lounging beside it with reading material (he's currently working through volume II of "Les Grands Courants de l'Histoire Universelle" by Jacques Pirenne, which that historian, who was also the son of a historian, wrote over *12 years* from 1944-1956; a son who takes up the same profession as his father and perhaps badly wants to live up the paternal standard — how unexpected an interest for Pierre).

Past pool reads have included Balzac's *Comédie Humaine* – which he finished in two years, the memoirs of philosopher Henri de Saint-Simon , the works of Thomas Mann that had somehow escaped his attention earlier in life and a good deal more of history, particularly texts of Egyptology.

Pierre has practically a full head of greyish-white hair and a trim beard of the same two interspersed colors. What wrinkles and crinkles he has at the corners of his eyes seem to convey not haggardness but heightened attention, as if he's listening intently to your every word – and judging its aptness, its quality, as you go.

Upon first view, the house seems more cottage than castle, its construction in 1850 not immediately apparent (the trees dotting the perimeter of the property have been growing since that year, too).

But still, the whole moment is surreal – for myself, for Shyam. I know this because we keep exchanging looks of wonder – the writer who's finally meeting the subject of a year and a half of research, the perfumer who's meeting one of her industry's most highly-regarded figures (who was additionally considered unreachable and bitter – almost a Salinger-esque recluse who'd turned his back on the perfumery world of the present).

We're kindly escorted in, past a kitchen to which we'll repair for lunch not too much later and a centuries-old gorgeous mosaic floor whose brownish-red and green flourishes seem somehow diminished by the presence just above them of my grey suede Pumas.

Kathy having stayed in the kitchen to put away the gifted victuals – or perhaps to tend to that upcoming lunch – Pierre alone leads Shyam and me into two adjacent rooms that Pierre has turned into his own "cabinet of curiosities."

These are overwhelming rooms, so bursting with eclectic, historic, odd items I've no idea what to scan first – I forget whatever initial questions I wanted to ask. Of his design principles, Pierre says he has "decorated in the romantic style [by utilizing] all the collections that I have accumulated during my life."

Judging from the results, one can immediately tell it hasn't been a boring one.

The first room, which Pierre has dedicated to scientific objects, has pinstriped wallpaper from which emerge the heads of animals (Pierre doesn't hunt, except that is for these strange objects at antique fairs, which he attends regularly). There are lizards pinned to the ceiling. Shelves and cabinetry covered in insects, fossils, minerals.

But it's the second (non-life-science) chamber to which we are led to sit.

Here, a gorgeous wooden cabinet is topped by a very baroque-looking cuckoo clock. A table at the room's center is wood covered by a massive stone slab (is it marble? I wonder). Above that, hanging from the ceiling, is a black and gold chandelier.

Pierre, unfazed by his own home, asks for our drink orders – I simply tell him I'll have what he's having, which turns out to be a screwdriver. A choice totally amenable to me – and perhaps one well calibrated by Pierre – but which threatens a nightmarish start to the day when the legend returns from the bar with my drink and, somehow lacking in even basic motor skills, I spill not a small amount of it as soon as I raise it to my lips.

Did I mention the room's fancy, aged floral rug, which is lying beneath me?

Shyam, sitting in a plush, suede red chair with a white runner down the middle and a fringed border of red fabric at the base, notices what I've done. Her eyes express the horror I already feel deeply in my gut. She looks at me as though I've just singlehandedly grabbed a car wheel and tried to crash it from the passenger seat – maybe not out of malice but most definitely out of momentary madness.

I look up at Pierre to see whether he took in the horrendous levy-breach/failed-imbibing himself, but he's either the most incredibly kind host I've yet encountered, faking inattention, or somehow my orange juice overflow escaped his gaze in actuality.

If the latter is true, it may yet to be topped by a greater miracle, one of which I learn very slowly and subtly, as I gradually let my eyes shift downward, toward the rug:

All of the OJ has landed on those aforementioned Puma sneakers. They are soaked, but a size 12 was sufficient to keep the expensive warp and weft beneath 'em clean as a whistle.

The relief I feel is monumental.

Which means I can now eye the rest of the room, as Pierre sits nearby, legs crossed and engages Shyam and me in those first ice-breaker moments of in-person conversation.

Pierre in his domain.

The walls are covered in centuries-old portraits of anonymous humans, including 100 miniatures. A music stand features yellowed sheet music from an Edward Elgar composition ("Land of Hope and Glory").

One table features innumerable seals – the handles ivory, the metal ends flat and very inviting (I want to ink these bottoms and press hard onto sheets of paper to see what marks would appear; given my OJ exploits, however, I don't ask Pierre whether I may).

Every little counter and niche features an ornate candlestick. And then, behind a couch, there's this folding screen that resembles a wooden garden trellis and is covered in what I assume is fake ivy but, hell, might be real, who knows?

But one of my favorite touches occurs somewhat out of sight – in a place one could never look except during its seasons of disuse, such as now, in the heat of late spring, days away from the start of summer:

Inside the fireplace, the interior slabs of cement (or whatever material accompanies the stone) are decorated in golden *fleur de lis*. I recognize France is where the symbol originated, but it feels as though I've discovered a small portal secretly outfitted by a New Orleans native when nobody was looking. A Superdome touch in a corner of a castle.

I'm not even sure where to find them, but Pierre has told me the room contains Neapolitan gouaches brought back to France centuries ago by aristocratic travelers who'd taken pan-continental grand tours. The windows are draped in a parted slate-blue satin curtain.

Above a gorgeous bureau filled with books are what appear to be two gas lamps – and I can immediately see the great appeal of reading in this room beneath that sort of warm, sooty light (but as they have plugs coming out of them, I'd say this particular pair has been modified).

Eventually, Kathy joins us in the sitting room and from there till the end of the visit the conversation ranges over so many topics I can hardly keep up (and is this even real?). Reflecting on the couple years I spent as a screenwriter, Pierre says there's no shame in writing for the screen. In the winter, he likes to watch a couple old films a day, but even just other night, he and Kathy had watched again Bogie and Bacall in "The Big Sleep." Pierre was struck by the dialogue, so he looked online to see who had penned it.

Faulkner contributed to that script, Pierre says – no shame in trying your hand at a form Falkner did. And then Kathy chimes in – or maybe this is still Pierre – that Fitzgerald wrote for the screen, too (though with somewhat less success, I say, but gently).

Eventually we move into the open kitchen-dining area for a summery salad-seafood combo. I'd be doing the dish an injustice to describe it, except to say that it's dressed in mangos and that seems to be the tangy key.

Pierre, Kathy and Shyam at lunch.

I find it hard to isolate any one topic from the lunch – it was neither so raucous nor boozy that I should perceive it all as a wonderful, if constituently indiscernible, haze, but there is the matter of adrenaline, that rush that imparts a liveliness to events but also, in making them transcendent, renders them near-impossible to recapture via regular faculties.

I know we talked about old times – crazy perfume doings Pierre and Kathy know well from memory and I from dedicated study. The Roure crowd, the Takasago office, the students who had heart and one in particular who faked it, who betrayed Pierre in a way he never thought a former pupil would. I won't name that relatively well-known perfumer here – Pierre and Kathy would prefer to let that episode be. In fact, as a result of this request, I've not included the perfumer on any page of this book – not even once.

(I did ask them one last time via email if they might elaborate on the nature of this betrayal. Their emailed reply: "Suffice it to say he had a very good teacher.")

What I do most definitely recall:

Kathy says she is wary of any quest to avenge the wrongdoings Olivier Creed perpetrated against Pierre (and Herault and Rasquinet and a few others, though Pierre was the primary target of Creed's office insinuations).

Yes, Olivier paid Pierre, for the work that made the enterprise worth nearly a billion dollars to its recent buyer, just a few tailored suits. And no major bonus as promised. But even if these perfumers couldn't see that incredibly lucrative end result in Olivier's favor, did they not know, if they searched their hearts in those moments, that they were being abused? Were they not adult enough to say so?

I come from a world of bylines, I reply. It's that simple. You don't sign your name to another reporter's work. You don't take away another's claim to posterity. And if you're going to, you'd better bloody compensate the hardworking mothereffer.

Somehow the topic of romance comes up, and Kathy, while prepping dessert, compares the Roure love triangle of the early 1980s – when Pierre fell for her while still married to perfumer Francoise Caron – to the Prince Charles-Lady Di-Camilla Parker Bowles affair – quoting verbatim Diana, who so famously in a 1995 TV interview with Martin Bashir said, "There were three of us in this marriage."

As Kathy does so, I wonder, despite finding her a hoot, whether she quite realizes the implication of that comparison – as Pierre was married to Francoise, that means Kathy wasn't Diana – beloved by the world, universally considered a wronged party – but Camilla, a somewhat less-appreciated figure.

Regardless, it's a bold thing to say. I come to appreciate this about Kathy: the brassy candor that fills in all those quiet moments when Pierre would prefer to ruminate (before ultimately reaching a judgment, it seems, in accordance with Kathy's in the first place).

After lunch, per Kathy's suggestion and his agreement, Pierre leads us up a carpeted spiral staircase, which curves around a chandelier at its center and features endless paintings hung from the floor to ceiling on its outer boundary, the wall to our right.

A slim rectangular window halfway up lets in light, over which the Bourdons have arranged a canvas of a small town in winter, all overcast bluish-grays above and muddy, dispiriting browns and greens below. A shed in the foreground topped with snow like pastry icing is cleverly crossed by a thin, blackish cathedral spire in the back – such a slim, sinister form. All the paint has been applied roughly, a wintry scene with hints of pure geometry.

A warm day fit for a swim outside – but here's a still life by Giorgio Morandi (in terms of abstract solidity of the shapes) crossed with a bracing, unforgivingly Belichikian New England winter and the palette of a Winslow Homer.

Several steps further up we reach a more remarkable (if a slightly-less-enjoyable-to-expound-upon indulgently) milieu – Pierre's second-floor office, which is covered in cheetah-print carpet and whose far side features windows looking out onto the green expanse of the backyard, each penned in by curling, Parisian-balcony-like grates and overhung with similarly *metropolitain* striped awning.

It is this room – more even than his makeshift museum below us, his cabinets of curiosities – that proves the most shocking in the house, for reasons that will be momentarily clear.

First, the books and papers.

There are the expected shelves of books, some rare – including very old and historic editions of Proust's "La Recherche." There are Kathy's valuable vintage Barbie dolls, still in their boxes. Beneath a magnifying glass, a letter from Frederic Bourdelier, the "brand culture and heritage director" of Parfums Dior and a more recent graduate of Pierre's alma mater, Sciences Po.

The shelves feature histories of French interior design, Western dress from antiquity to the present, a million biographies of Pierre's political hero, Charles de Gaulle, including the two-volume series written by his son, Phillipe de Gaulle.

There are volumes by Malraux, Andre Lalande, Henri Bergson, Barthes, Claude Levi-Strauss, Sophocles, Nietzsche. I forget to ask Pierre about the provenance of an Asian book whose spine features in gold the image of an older man, some wizened and thoughtful elder, whose long beard eventually curls upward, forming above him what appears a cloud of incense.

There are two stately wooden pedestal desks with gold-bordered leather inlays – one features a laptop, a cigar box and photos of Kathy as a young woman of 19 or 20 or so. Pierre motions toward it at one point and says, Can I not see why he was immediately and overwhelmingly smitten when he first noticed her in Jean Amic's office at Roure – why he was trucked, gobsmacked?

Regardless of the truth, in any such circumstance – that is, a man holding up photos of his former lover and current spouse inside his home – I would say, *Yes, gorgeous.* On the other hand, while it feels perfectly okay for a Frenchman to pick up a frame and say, *Look at this undeniable beauty,* it occurs to me even within a split second that such words will sound far less suave leaving my louder and more aggressive American mouth. They'd seem rude, reductive, and, worst of all, in a way, for a writer, inartistic and uncouth.

The line between appreciation and objectification is shockingly thin and far from unmoving for a tourist; also, I know such praise of a woman at an earlier stage of life kinda implies that the current version has lost something, which would never be my intention or even my belief – I come from the world of boxing – I know we're all in the process of building ourselves up only to be torn apart again, nobody of any gender escapes decay, so why not acknowledge it (more or less)?

But all those considerations aside: Pierre ain't wrong. In one photo Kathy looks down, large white-framed sunglasses perched upon her scalp, and the camera captures what seems a minor state of perturbation, but hers is such a winsome frown I can't help but want to cheer her. In the other, she looks straight at the photographer, lush, dark hair past her shoulders framing her almost-confrontational face. *What do you think you see?* she seems to be saying, less impish than precocious, knowing, with a snarl.

Gorgeous, I say. *She's gorgeous.*

I don't even recall Pierre smiling or nodding – I think he knew already the truth so well his mind had moved on to other things; he'd questioned me without waiting for answer, like a sharpshooter, a Steph Curry, who turns around and begins the run back up-court after launching one, utterly secure before the ball has swished through the net that it undoubtedly will.

Meanwhile, at my feet is a small wooden magazine rack, such as you might find in a doctor's waiting room, with vintage magazines – of Paris Match, of publications related to interior design.

But it's the contents of his non-writing desk with which Pierre astounds Shyam and instigates me. First, there's the bound volume on its right side – a copy of the never-released novel Pierre wrote after retiring from perfumery – *"L'Homme Aux Mille Parfums"* – or, "The Man with a Thousand Fragrances" – inspired by the life of Pierre's mentor, Edmond Roudnitska.

I know Pierre has written such a book and, moreover, that it seemed it might be published by the respected French house Robert Laffont, until one of its editors decided suddenly such a text could interest only those already enamored of fragrance.

Yes, Pierre thought at the time, that's the point – this is a book for perfume lovers, of whom there remain quite a few in France alone. "Suddenly, I gave up and no longer showed it to publishers," Pierre told me of his course following that initial disappointment. "I did not want to renew the adventure of Cool Water, refused eight times."

These words echo in me as Pierre pulls out a thick, old, weathered notebook for Shyamala's perusal, filled with a neat and unrelenting French cursive – the notes Pierre has taken for decades on every material and composition he has smelled. Ever.

As he gives Shyam time to page through it – and how can she? I mean, where does she start and where does she stop? how to absorb something so rich without any preamble, without any time to prepare oneself and with the knowledge the party will move on to another topic or part of the property soon? – Pierre begins to explain the various glass bottles on his desk.

He has all of the latest raw materials here, he says, including captives from Firmenich, which intrigue Shyam herself can neither acquire nor use (as she works for rival firm Givaudan; naturally, she's interested in sniffing these).

And then comes the bigger surprise for Shyam, though I already know what's coming and if I've omitted it heretofore it was only to enhance the drama of this moment:

Pierre hasn't just been noodling around with compositions no one will ever smell, though he does that, too: When his longtime Austrian client and current pal Roland Kohl requests a new fragrance now and again for a home shopping network line called "Judith Williams," Pierre happily complies, formulating an entirely new scent. He sends his formulas for compounding to the old Grasse materials firm Jean Niel. "Sometimes the result amazes me myself," Pierre had told me months earlier. "It looks like I haven't lost my hand. After all, I must have been a good perfumer."

It's at this moment – give or take several minutes – when I decide finally to give Pierre a piece of my mind (although it's not really the first such instance and won't be the last).

This fear of failure you have, it's ridiculous, I say. So what that your father helped run Parfums Dior – did he ever formulate anything? Why quake at his opinion – why lend it such weight when the entire world esteems your creations? And Davidoff Cool Water has become legendary – are eight rejections really so hurtful that you can't feel them negated by the huge subsequent acceptance? Submit that novel you wrote to a million more publishers. My own writing is rejected far more than merely once before it's ever published, if it's ever published at all. It took like 20 tries for me to get anyone to put out my boxing book. And I'll tell you something else: You're so scared of failure that you're channeling a great love of perfumery into a venture the world cannot appreciate. These Judith Williams perfumes, only available via home shopping network in Germany and Austria, these are a cop-out. Let the wider world at least have the chance to sample your work. You're good enough, you're worth so much to the larger scent world. Why deprive us? Why not go for it big yet again? What could you really lose?

Was my speech exactly that long, are these the precise words I used? Probably not. I wasn't recording the office encounter. But my memory, however fallible it may be, says I put up a decent stand, in favor of taking creative risks instead of being ruled by fear. I don't recall Pierre saying anything in return, merely shrugging.

He is far more animated in an entirely French discussion with Shyam about materials and perfumery, before we go back downstairs and then outside for a constitutional around the property's perimeter, beneath its canopy of tree branches, alongside the river.

Shyam, sensitive to how much time Pierre has given her, generously walks ahead of him, to pair off with Kathy separately, so that I might chat once with the master in privacy before we go. What happens next is so befuddling I still can't quite unpack it on the car ride back.

I ask Pierre about the origins of his interest in Egyptology and he talks about the way Christian mythology could be said to have descended from the stories of Egypt.

Then asks me whether I am a Jew.

This being France, he is the third perfume industry person to ask me this within the span of a week (and all the inquisitors are sources I consider friends).

It's amazing if hardly unexpected, I think, that the French still find these bald-faced questions acceptable. Who cares what the answer is – does it affect my olfaction that I enjoy in the morning damn salty lox?

But Pierre immediately shifts my focus.

He says he had a relative named Sara, and he thinks he might be a Jew through her, and he likes visiting synagogues, and the persecution of the Jews meant they could carry and take with them only their learning and knowledge, which means they prize the same invisible, beautiful things that hold all the world's meaning for him. Study. Ideas. The word.

They couldn't carry anything with them, he says again.

It's the repetition of this line that spurs me to tell him my own grandfather, on a death march from an Austrian labor camp to the concentration camp Mauthausen, was also forced to move along without any items at all.

Except he was a braver soul than I'll ever be and didn't comply with this order, so when a fellow from his hometown collapsed during the march, my grandfather and great uncle helped lift him from the road, at the risk of being shot and left for dead in a roadside ditch right then and there, and carried this weak boy to the gates of the camp where he ended up reuniting with his father.

My grandfather carried something with him alright – a human who wound up surviving and immigrating to Canada and becoming a math professor in Toronto. A professor with whom my grandfather, thanks to the ingenious online sleuthing of my cousin, was reunited a half-century later.

That much he carried with him, my grandfather.

And I begin to weep.

I apologize, and he says, *No, it's okay, it's on me, I brought it up. You know, I wondered who you were, this American kid who said he was writing a perfume book. I had my doubts. But we know each other now. You're on the inside. Please come back whenever. You're invited always.*

I tell him I love him, I dash inside to take a piss and Shyam and I climb back into the Mini Cooper for a long, traffic-troubled trip back south to Paris.

I don't know how to describe to Shyam any of what has just happened. And soon small bickering about where we are and which exits to take dominates the discourse. We are tired and worn out upon the return to the Agnes Varda's Rue Daguerre. I feel nauseated from the way Shyam has ridden the brake. She's stressed by all the humans and Vespas who have streamed around the car during rush hour in the heart of the city (she turns on Sufjan Stevens to soothe us both – *all things go, all things* go). When I exit the Mini finally, I slam the door with an unfair fury.

We will make up later.

For now, it's impossible to believe I've been gone for just a single day. It occurs to me as I pack for my return flight to New York the following morning that perhaps I should never take Pierre up on his word – no subsequent encounter will be as heartfelt and magical, bittersweet and poignant, as this first. Anything else I say or do will somehow diminish the intensity-purity-success of this first in-person encounter.

It occurs to me, too, that Pierre didn't merely underline his own devotion to the book but the reason why this first volume should make him protagonist to Creed's opposite – I've interviewed 50 perfumers. Their stories are varied and fascinating. And it's not that Pierre has abjured objects, that's he's some ascetic or strange recluse. He told me months before I'd ventured to his chateau:

"I follow Honoré de Balzac's advice, who in *'Petites Misères de la Vie Conjugale'* has one of his protagonists say: 'Life cannot be started again, you have to fill it with pleasures.'"

It's simply that he can describe the philosophy with such a quote, that his life in perfumery has always been animated and annotated by the well-chosen words of others. He's a ghostwriter who treasures words for a fraudulent perfumer who, by all indications, doesn't.

What writer doesn't selfishly choose to focus on such a reader?

When I return to America, a perfumer who makes clones asks me whether I can connect him to Pierre. Offers to pay Pierre far more for these formulas he's sending to the German-Austrian home shopping folks than whatever he's currently receiving.

It's not about the money, I say, *and anyway, I tried convincing him to go big again, to submit his best for the world's consumption.*

And I realize while saying it that suddenly I don't want to spur Pierre to do anything larger anyway. Rather, I'd kindly ask any and all perfume fans, if you should find yourselves in Germany or Austria, tune into whichever channel has folks hawking *tchotchkes* on it and simply wait for the beauty products to be featured. Place an order when you hear the words "Judith Williams."

This is the only tribute for which Pierre has asked. And quixotic though it may be, it should be respected – perhaps especially for being quixotic.

Someone has to tilt at windmills while others sell companies for a billion dollars.[74]

Acknowledgments

Dan Kirschen: I had an inchoate idea and you brought it together – found its most compelling element and urged me to concentrate on it. I'm a better person and writer for that brilliant maneuver and for our partnership as a whole. You're a helluva dude and a *sensei*, to boot.

Paul Hendrickson: You tried to hook me up with all the people who could make this book a reality. That those attempts never quite panned out I'm sorry, but I hope in realizing it anyway I've created something of which you can be proud. Always my work will be somewhat attributable to you – my byline also yours. You're a good man and a brave one, and I hope what I do reflects those values even a little bit. I try. And I love ya.

Jamie-Lee Josselyn: I can't quite describe the tremendous sense of fulfillment afforded me by my visits to your classroom — only that they leave me high and giddy, convinced, however momentarily, that even if my own work should fall short, I might yet make it through one of your students. I thank you for these moments of potential propagation, for permitting me to dream of a vicarious fulfillment in the otherwise fearsome future. Thank you making the passage of time so much less scary. And, above all of that, for being the best friend and mentor a kid-turned-guest-speaker could ever desire.

Marlene Glazer and the Lippmann family: You treat me as one of your own even when you're mired in protracted battles that would wear out completely any normal persons. I don't know you do it, but I thank you for it — for the seriousness with which you take the onetime-tutor's ambition and output. Always I'll try to make Chappaqua proud, as a result. Always.

Sam Goldberg — always been the best editor of my work, always will be. This whole thing is mighty-improved for your having combed through it so very carefully. Peace, love, and hummus.

I couldn't have created this book without the cooperation of the fragrance industry and its many kind, if occasionally guarded, perfumers, scientists, executives, archivists and critics, including:

Abdulla Ajmal, Agnes Webster, Akiko Kamei, Alienor Massenet, Ammar Atmeh, Andy Tauer, Ann Gottlieb, Anne Flipo, Anne-Marie Saget, Antoine Lie, Antoine Maisondieu, Aurelien Guichard, Bernard Ellena, Bruno Jovanovic, Calice Becker, Caroline Sabas, Cecile Zarokian, Celine Barel, Chantal Roos, Christian Provenzano, Christophe Laudamiel, Clara and John Molloy, Clare Finn, Claude Dir, Dale Dewey, Damien Stammers, Dan Naughton, David Apel, Dominique Ropion, Domitille Michalon-Bertier, Dr. Luis Saraiva, Dr. Michael Lankin, EJ Wells, Elisabeth Carre, Emilie Bevierre-Coppermann, Fabrice Pellegrin, Francesca Bianchi, Franco Wright and Adam Eastwood, Frank Voelkl, Fred Jacques, George Zaharoff, Geza Schoen, Giles Gordon, Guillaume Flavigny, Hamid Merati-Kashani, Harry Fremont, Honorine Blanc, Ilias Ermenidis, Jean-Christophe Herault, Jean-Claude Ellena, Jean-Louis Sieuzac, Jean-Marc Chaillan, Jerome Di Marino, Jerome Herrgott, Dr. Johan Lundstrom, Joy Amin, Juliette Karagueuzoglou, Kuno Somner, Laurent Le Guernec, Laurice Rahme, Lucas Sieuzac, Mackenzie Reilly, Mark Behnke, Mark Buxton, Mathieu Nardin, Melissa Lerma, Michael Edwards, Michael Simpson, Mike Paulle, Miriam Mirani, Natasha Cote, Nathalie Feisthauer, Navin Ullal, Nicolas Beaulieu, Olivier Gasche, Olivier Gillotin, Olivier Pescheux, Pascal Gaurin, Pierre-Constantin Gueros, Pissara Umavijani, Ralf Schwieger, Raymond Chaillan, Raymond Matts, Roger Schmid, Rosendo Mateu, Shyamala Maisondieu, Sidonie Lancesseur, Sonia Constant, Sylvaine Delacourte, Thierry Wasser, Trudi Loren, Ugo Charron, Victor Wong, Vincent Kuczinski, Xavier Renard, Yves Cassar, and of course, Pierre and Kathleen Bourdon.

And thanks to these inspirational inventors of non-olfactive oratory: Carlo Rotella, Jim Lampley, Mike Woods, Romy Oltuski.

Harry Fremont — the week I spent on your Sonoma property was edifying and encouraging. There was real meaning to our final day removal of that vetiver root from the earth (not to mention the late-night, wine-facilitated discussions of my dating life). You are more friend to me than subject and always will be — though I hope in subsequent books to highlight your incredible rise through the industry — and the oh-so-lovable manner that — allied with your talent — no doubt helped facilitate it.

More on Nathalie Feisthauer – the perfumer who first took me seriously, whose tremendous talent is perhaps underappreciated in a community fixated on future deadlines and very rarely concerned with what might have been. A generous and beautiful teacher when I needed just that, and a friend when I needed that, too.

Who saw through me, who read between my emailed lines, who understood my limitations even when I chose not to express them. Nat, I hope you'll read this and think: That kid did alright by us, he played fair, he loved truly. He really did like my rooftop barbecue (I definitely did).

Hey, Shyamala, more on you, too: You were giving and open-minded and creative in ways I found inspiring routinely. I probably gave up on writing this a handful of times only to receive an email from you, poetic and sincere, that spurred me to take up the project again.

It'd be insufficient to say this book wouldn't exist without you, as that's perhaps true of a few people. It's perhaps more precise to say, I wouldn't want it to – your whole being, luminous, thoughtful, quiet, made me want to craft the text such that it reflected those qualities. That didn't quite work out, as I'm a boisterous fool – but I see in its best parts, in certain sentences, that I've perhaps on rare occasion maybe-almost-nearly achieved it. Why are you such a superior storyteller? It's not like I can write the formula for Oud Minerale.

Jean-Claude: If I had known you no longer play the flute, I would've chosen another early X-mas gift. All the same, I hope the *shinobue* testifies to my tremendous gratitude for all of your help, especially your connecting me to the star of this story, the man at the center of Part I. That move vaulted me inside the castle walls (almost literally). I know my language isn't so clever as to have enabled my finagling there without serious assistance. Which you provided in spades.

Judith Gross and Robert Fridovich and Sophie Cauchie: You set up the engagements and encounters without which I'd be infinitely less-informed. Thank you for opening the doord and inviting me in when you just as easily could've closed 'em hard on my face (thus bruising my beak into a Durante-wide bulb). *Merci beaucoup.*

Luca Turin: Your approval humbled me (made me feel ill, as if I were somehow a fraud, because the real me could never earn such praise). But your friendship means more. Wherever you are in the world – Greece, the UK, a future moon colony – I hope we never stop talking cars (#Giugiaro).

Matthew Leish — thanks for being my keen legal eagle.

Harold Aspis — you're the sweetest *shul* socializer Scarsdale has — or ever will — but I thank you not for your commitment to the community but to me. Your confidence that I'd produce the work I envisioned, your reminders that I had the faculties to figure it all out no matter my personal problems— these not-so-small acts of generosity stayed with me and sustained me at moments when perhaps we weren't even in touch. When perhaps you had no idea I was contemplating your words. And so I hope my own words validate yours, prove your belief in me was well-founded all along.

Orly— You convinced me on a lawn to go with this story; your instincts, unfailingly right, proved so again. I hope I did the idea justice. I can't thank you enough for the confidence boosts, critiques, pre-nuptial commentaries on Guerlain and Parfums de Marly offerings, and just the general way you let your knowledge of me inform your feedback. Keen and caring of ya. Let's do it again.

As this section's titled "Acknowledgments," I want to put writing temporarily aside and acknowledge the lone thing more important than meaningful work: love — both that offered up by my family and that which I give to and receive from the peers I prize.

That means Avi, Maia, Elisha, Judah, Boston-to-Baltimore Miriam, Jersey-Seattle Miriam, Ari, Adam, Brad, Joe, all the Aubreys (even that darn pooch), Becher and Jose, to name but a small few (it's weird that as I write this, I seem less misanthropic than I thought myself to be; I suppose I'm schizoid in my relations with other humans, whom I alternately consider indispensable and overwhelming). Regardless, it's a helluva crew, or as Carly Simon might put it, *Nobody does it better* (#TheSpyWhoLovedMe #Cosmos).

Claire: The desire to make you happy such that you flash your incomparable smile has spurred me on in so many ways. It undoubtedly helped me power through a book already 1.25 pandemic years in the making. Thank you for the salmon, the crossword contributions, the cover design advice and sketches. Consider this the only knitting of which I am capable —the weaving-together of a tale — but a gift to ya just the same.

Ma, Pa, Jon: I don't just thank you for your assessment of this work in its finished state but for your evaluations during the earliest phases of is development — you were so very helpful, as we cohabited for 9 pandemic months, in helping me build the text up from nothing but a few hazy notions to a carefully-structured narrative. Thank you for tolerating my earsplitting Zoom interviews of Paris-based perfumers. Thanks for the shared viewing sessions each night on which I look back now rather fondly: The 7 pm "Jeopardy!" competitions, and later each evening, the Turkish soap opera showings.

We did pretty well, all in all.

I still don't really know what "Black Money Love" means – but I know I don't have to either – I don't even need to *Ask* (pun intended).

It was, for a period, ours.

Appendix (for the lost)

1979 - Hermes Eau D'Orange Verte (Francoise Caron)

1981- Ombre Rose by Jean-Charles Brosseau (Caron)

1981 - Yves Saint Laurent Kouros (Pierre Bourdon)

1982- Drakkar Noir for Guy Laroche (Pierre Wargnye)

1985- Creed Green Irish Tweed (Bourdon)

1986 - Hermes Bel Ami (Jean-Louis Sieuzac)

1986 - Zino Davidoff (Michel Almairac)

1988 - Davidoff Cool Water (Bourdon)

1989 - Joop! Homme (Bourdon)

1992 - Shiseido Feminite du Bois (Bourdon & Sheldrake)

1992 - Creed Erolfa (Bourdon)

1994 - Dior Dolce Vita (Bourdon)

1995 - Creed Silver Mountain Water (Bourdon)

1995 - Creed Millésime Impérial (Bourdon)

2005- Canali for men (Bourdon & Jean-Christophe Herault)

2005 - Creed Original Santal (Bourdon)

2009 - Canali dal 1934 (Herault)

2010- Creed Aventus (Herault)

2011 - Creed Royal Oud (Julien Rasquinet)

OIL HOUSES*

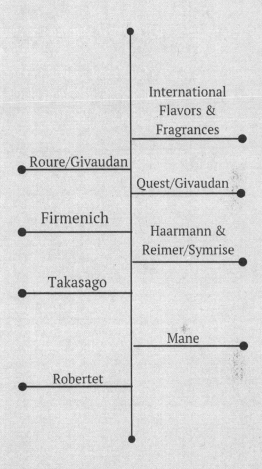

International
Flavors &
Fragrances

Roure/Givaudan

Quest/Givaudan

Firmenich

Haarmann &
Reimer/Symrise

Takasago

Mane

Robertet

*companies that employ
perfumers and make money by
selling the ingredients for
which their formulas call

+the acquiring house appears
after the slash

229

PIERRE'S OIL HOUSE JOURNEY,
in sequence

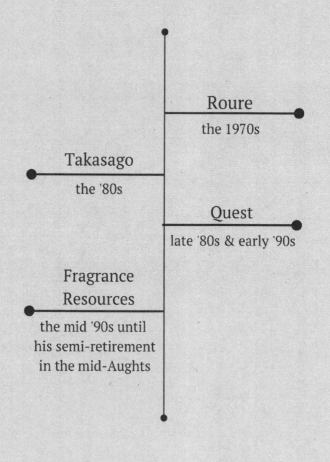

Roure
the 1970s

Takasago
the '80s

Quest
late '80s & early '90s

Fragrance
Resources

the mid '90s until
his semi-retirement
in the mid-Aughts

Notes

INTRODUCTION

1   "Sniffing the Air with: Olivier Creed; A Nose With a Stomach for New York," The New York Times, Feb. 7, 1999.

2   Much of the following material is derived from: "Monsieur Olivier Creed Sniffs Out a Living," New York Observer, Sept. 20, 1999.

3   Olivier told Forbes in October 1999 that the company generates $40 million in annual revenue, with a profit margin of 12 percent. This is almost certainly an intentional diminishment of his margins so as to convince the Forbes reader of the extravagance of his costly natural ingredients. Mass perfumery can achieve margins of 90 percent on the juice. There's every reason to think Olivier can keep his nearly as high (I say nearly, because Creed can't achieve the same economies of scale as Coty or Lauder). At the time of the BlackRock acquisition two decades later, analysts estimated Creed's annual revenue at $200 million, a large portion of which could be straight-up profit

To get a sense of the complexities involved in these negotiations: Creed's Paris boutique, at 38 Avenue Pierre 1er de Serbie, near the Four Seasons, has been registered as its own limited liability company since January of 2006, under the name of Olivier's ex-wife, Fabienne. In 2019, this little shop, whose marble busts, carpeted stairs and ubiquitous mirrors recall a Vegas hotel, did $2.6 million in revenue, or 1-2 percent of the company's total intake. This backs up an additional truth about Creed known by those in the know: People in Paris have no longstanding relationship with these liquids. They've heard of Guerlain, sure, but Creed? It does not register as a legitimate Parisian institution – because, well, in its current form, it is not.

CHAPTER 1: WHAT IS PERFUME?

4   Actually, this is another odd manner of doing business shared by boxing and beauty (specifically, fine fragrance): in the former, the very best champs are siloed into systems so that two tremendous talents of identical size, perhaps each with a belt

and undefeated record, may never meet in the ring because one is signed to Top Rank and bound to appear on ESPN and another is a PBC fighter who may only appear on Showtime or Fox.

In beauty, the perfumers compete against each other to win briefs across companies – IFF perfumers may indeed face their counterparts at Givaudan or Symrise – but sometimes the results are in even before submissions have been presented.

These days, Firmenich perfumer Albert Morillas won't work on a brief unless he's guaranteed the right to formulate the entire lineup of which the present project is just one part. And in the case of Tom Ford, which is licensed by Lauder, the decision was made by Estee's protegees' protegees that it'd be better for all involved if Givaudan alone dominated that brand's submissions.

I believe there was a financial consideration to this decision – Swiss multinationals perhaps liking to incentivize favorable outcomes – but there is a legit artistic consideration, too: the conversations between Lauder ace nose Karyn Khoury and the Givaudan perfumers wer inherently more intimate than they'd be were further folks involved. Winning a Tom Ford brief was about figuring out what Karyn liked and why – a task that becomes increasingly manageable as the room empties – once you can look her in the eyes – and vice-versa.

5   "Men's Perfume Fashion Gets No Foothold Here," The New York Times, Oct. 22, 1933.

6   "Shulton, Inc." The New York Times, Feb. 17, 1965.

7   Stamford Advocate, "Stamford Vietnam soldier's duty of honor too worthy for pay," Nov. 24, 2018.

8   This attribution to Sulik is the work of Australian Michael Edwards, whose online fragrance database, though wildly expensive, is an essential reference for everyone in the industry.

CHAPTER 2: HOW PERFUMERY WORKS

9   The New York Times, not privy to the actual language, said the scent was "aimed at the woman who wanted to be feminine again." Meanwhile, there has always been some controversy over whether YSL actively targeted Lauder's Youth-Dew, and I think I've found the cause of the confusion. But in short, yes: I believe based on my research that Opium was intended to be a Gallic-styled dupe worthy of a Times Square street-walker.

Originally, Loic Delteil, who managed YSL perfumes, briefed just Jean Amic and Raymond Chaillan of Roure – Loic is the one who asked for the fragrance of a whore. Chaillan and colleague Francoise Marin were soon dispatched to the Roure office in Teaneck to begin the Franco-reworking of Youth-Dew, which had been reverse-engineered brilliantly by Roure's US nose Bob Slattery.

Chaillan developed an orange accord, utilizing the Firmenich ingredient Mandarinal, and introduced the formula's carnation note and myriad spices (including cloves, nutmeg, cinnamon, pepper, coriander and bay).

At this point, back in France, Jean-Louis Sieuzac took over the project and began altering Chaillan's formula, itself based on Slattery's reconstruction of Youth-Dew.

This later stage of development involving Sieuzac also included YSL's international marketing manager, Chantal Roos, who has always maintained, including in chats with me, she'd never heard of Youth-Dew until Opium's release. This is possible given Chantal's later entrance – but it meant the marketer was thereafter telling an incomplete story about Opium's meretricious and uninspired origin.

10   Cavallier, hired away from Firmenich by LVMH to be the in-house perfumer for Bvlgari's $300 line and all Louis Vuitton fragrances, utilized that raspberry again in 2018, in Louis Vuitton's Ombre Nomade, whose challenging oud-birch-smoke top resolves into the most gorgeous fruity drydown of perhaps any scent I've ever worn.

11   At least, according what Olivier himself told me he was told.

12   Guerlain's history is fascinating – but less so than the history to which it bore witness. See an Aug. 26, 1914, ad on page 5 of the New York Times for Gimbels department store. An ad published just after the Great War had broken out, though years before America would enter it. The Herald Square emporium promises not to raise rates on perfumes, in spite of European strife, including on several Guerlain favorites, such as Apree L'Ondee (still just $5.15) and Jicky ($2.70).

13   For instance, Derby was actually supposed to be a leather fragrance based on the concept of a Roman soldier, an idea fancied by Phillipe Guerlain, the firm's managing director and a history buff. It was called "Centurion" and glass bottles had already been made to resemble a centurion's dress when a man hired from Procter & Gamble, who had served there as a mere assistant product manager, successfully pressed Saget and perfumer Jean-Paul Guerlain to alter the top note to resemble Paco Rabanne pour Homme and changed the name of the juice to "Derby."

Somewhat hilariously – but also poignantly, as if a storied family firm were staging a final act of defiance as MBAs raided the place – the bottles couldn't be changed at that point, and thus emerged onto the shelves a glass vessel with a steely grey crap, a clever abstraction of an armor-clad ancient soldier of empire…with a totally inapt name across what would seem the sculpture's navel.

14 Les Echoes, "LUXE : Tout en maintenant son independance - Parfums: Creed veut sortir de la confidentialite," Nov. 30, 1993.

15 Town & Country, "The Smell of Money," Sept. 15, 2014.

16 The New York Times Magazine, "Still Going," Nov. 16, 1995.

CHAPTER 3: THE INHERITANCE OF OLIVIER CREED

17 "Creed, de père en fils depuis sept générations," Le Figaro, July 10, 2007.

18 "REWIND: Interview with Olivier CREED," https://www.cafleurebon.com/rewind-interview-with-oliver-creed/ June 5, 2010.

19 "TAILORED TWEED SUITS ARE SYNONYMOUS WITH EARLY SPRING," The New York Times, Feb. 6, 1938.

20 "Sixth scents: Olivier Creed, the world's most elegant perfumier, explains his art," The Independent, March 3, 2013.

21 "Creed, de père en fils depuis sept générations," Le Figaro, July 10, 2007.

22 "Sixth scents: Olivier Creed, the world's most elegant perfumier, explains his art," The Independent, March 3, 2013.

23 "Olivier Creed, Parfums Creed," Cosmétique Mag, May 2, 2019.

CHAPTER 4: THE EDUCATION OF PIERRE BOURDON

24 I. Wallrabenstein, J. Gerber, S. Rasche, I. Croy, S. Kurtenbach, T. Hummel, H. Hatt, The smelling of Hedione results in sex-differentiated human brain activity, NeuroImage,
Volume 113,
2015,
Pages 365-373,
ISSN 1053-8119,
https://doi.org/10.1016/j.neuroimage.2015.03.029.
(https://www.sciencedirect.com/science/article/pii/S1053811915002116)

Abstract: A large family of vomeronasal receptors recognizes pheromone cues in many animals including most amphibia, reptiles, rhodents, and other mammals. Humans possess five vomeronasal-type 1 receptor genes (VN1R1–VN1R5), which code for proteins that are functional in recombinant expression systems. We used two different recombinant expression systems and identified Hedione as a ligand for the putative human pheromone receptor VN1R1 expressed in the human olfactory mucosa. Following the ligand identification, we employed functional magnetic resonance imaging (fMRI) in healthy volunteers to characterize the in vivo action of the VN1R1 ligand Hedione. In comparison to a common floral odor (phenylethyl alcohol), Hedione exhibited significantly enhanced activation in limbic areas (amygdala, hippocampus) and elicited a sex-differentiated response in a hypothalamic region that is associated with hormonal release. Utilizing a novel combination of methods, our results indicate that the putative human pheromone receptor VN1R1 is involved in extra-olfactory neuronal activations induced by the odorous substance Hedione. The activation of VN1R1 might play a role in gender-specific modulation of hormonal secretion in humans.

Keywords: Social odors; Hedione; Pheromones; fMRI; Olfaction; Human VN1R1

25 Forty years later, I'd interview his son, Jean-Marc Chaillan, who'd end up becoming a perfumer for International Flavors & Fragrances in New York and the author of Aramis Tobacco Reserve, which he wears himself on night excursions and which I donned the night before I got my second Covid vaccine shot (don't ask me why – the nose knows what it wants without betraying that reason to consciousness).

26 "Smelling Good Costly for Men," The New York Times, June 10, 1978.

27 "Smelling Good Costly for Men," The New York Times, June 10, 1978.

28 "Smelling Good Costly for Men," The New York Times, June 10, 1978.

29 Synarome's US boss in the 1980s – a former collegiate basketball player who wound up playing pro in Europe – lived during that decade in a ramshackle penthouse formerly occupied by Damon Runyan, which overlooked the old Eighth Avenue site of the Garden. His name was Mike Paulle, and he was an old school PR man in the PT Barnum mold. When Geraldine Ferraro became an '84 vice-presidential candidate, he commissioned a juice in her name, which drew media attention (hell, he publicized his historic, if now slightly dingy, apartment in order to score an article in the New York Times). Paulle would later date a perfumer at IFF and, after messing that relationship up, move to Vegas and become the media director for the World Series of Poker).

30 https://perfumersupplyhouse.com/product/animalis-1745-3-synarome/

31 The fuller party story: Saint Laurent, whose eponymous beauty line was then owned by Charles of the Ritz – the company begun 60 years earlier by a hairstylist at New York's Ritz Hotel named Charles Jundt – commissioned Rudolf Nureyev

to dance in three ballets.

A "Kouros" in ancient Greece was a statue of a naked young man placed either in a temple, in a dedication to the gods, or at a gravesite, and the YSL festivities were dotted with replicas thereof. Catherine Deneuve and dancer Zizi Jeanmaire attended, as well as the editors of Vogue, Playboy and Harper's Bazaar — all flown in on Charles of the Ritz's dime.

The Nureyev dancing was done to the music of the Monte Carlo Symphony (also flown in) at the Opera Comique theater. After the ballet, the invitees were chauffeured in limousines to Maxim's to supp.

Women's Wear Daily columnist Louise Esterhazy documented the way the guests were subdivided in the eatery. How piddling journalists were condemned to the basement. How even the editor of French Vogue was asked by Yves to abandon her prime seat near the man himself and re-position herself on the third floor, or what she termed the "attic."

Yves himself bailed on the party early but not before being photographed as if in ad for his own product – laughing conspiratorially with a woman we can't quite identify – whose celebrity is nevertheless assured – the observer, teased, wanting badly to know what was said – this desire leading to the greater one, a yearning to attend – all before a towering Greek nude sculpture.

CHAPTER 6: FAUSTUS

32   According to Pierre.

CHAPTER 7: THE KING

33   https://www.upi.com/Archives/1931/04/15/Spanish-Republicans-form-new-go vernment-as-King-Alfonso-flees-into-secret-exile/3101803371941/

34   "The Sweet Smell of Excess," Forbes, Oct. 10, 1999.

35   The brief pointed to Lancome's 1967 masculine, Balafre, whose name and marketing invoked a scarred (balafre) Catholic Duke known for his wars against Protestants. Carles wanted the new release to allude to an episode no less layered and notorious – that two decades had passed – that the initial concept seemed to treat religious violence rather flippantly – seem not to have mattered.

36   "pssssssssst!" The Dallas Morning News, March 25, 2001.

37   KNOW + TELL; Pg. 62, Details, December, 2008. "Spoil Them Silly Bath & Beauty,"

Daily News (New York), November 24, 2002. "Get into the St. Patrick's Day spirit from head to toe," The San Francisco Chronicle, March 13, 2005. "A perfume expert unbottles the mystique of scents," The New Zealand Herald, Dec. 13, 2011.

38 "Chanel makes a big pitch for a new perfume aimed at young women, its toughest market," The New York Times, Aug. 15, 2002.

39 https://kafkaesqueblog.com/tag/fragrance-sales-revenues/

40 "Benckiser set for future expansion," Cosmetics International, Sept. 25, 1992.

41 "Fragrance Foundation reports slow start to Christmas 1992," Cosmetics International, Feb. 25, 1993.

42 For what brief was Millésime Impérial devised?

"I no longer remember the origins of Millésime Impérial, Erolfa and [some other perfumes] that Olivier adopted on the same principle — by throwing himself on my left behinds," Pierre told me.

43 "The Sweet Smell of Excess," Forbes, Oct. 10, 1999.

44 "A Dab of Fig Tree Behind the Ear, Perhaps?" The New York Times, Dec. 28, 1997.

CHAPTER 8: THE CASTLES

45 "Claude Lévi-Strauss, 100, Dies; Altered Western Views of the 'Primitive,'" The New York Times, Nov. 4, 2009.

CHAPTER 9: AMBITION

46 "14 Famous Women and Their Favorite Perfumes," Town & Country, Nov. 23, 2016. "Take your pick of these flowery goods," Postmedia Breaking News, April 15, 2016. "Elegance Defined; In an Age of Indulgence, Audrey Hepburn Looks Even Better," Hartford Courant, Sept. 29, 2006.

47 This is the reason Pierre knew he couldn't properly compete with young-perfumer-on-the-rise Francis Kurkdjian for the Jean-Paul Gaultier Le Male brief: To him, it was a clear invitation to create something in the vein of Joop! Homme. As that was Pierre's own creation, he decided he'd rather submit something far different and lose than copy himself to win.

Kurkdjian had no such personal history with which to wrestle. Chantal Roos, who briefed the perfumers on this project and helped pick the winner, declined to comment on whether she wanted something Joop-esque. But having vaulted Francis to the top of the industry – where he's remained ever since through his own ingenuity – she feels entitled to call the now-star nose "my little Francis" no matter his fame.

48   "Creed Celebrates Its Past and Future," Women's Wear Daily, Dec. 10, 2010.

49   "Les plus vieilles familles d'artisans de Paris; Nez de père en fils," Le Figaro, Feb. 21, 1998.

CHAPTER 10: THE HUSTLER

50   It's both fascinating and depressing how comparatively excellent the October 1999 issue of Esquire in which the Jasmin ad appears is relative to current editions (and a great vindication of the editorial team longtime editor David Granger had assembled in just two years and would continue to employ for another 17 before being unceremoniously dumped by Hearst in 2016 as the entire industry scapegoated talented editors for the loss of ad revenue to the Internet): There's a cover-profile of George Clooney, who's just 38 years old, in advance of the release of the film "Three Kings"; an excellent Tom Junod profile of Hillary Clinton as she attempts to win a senate seat by canvassing rural New York and a previously-unpublished Raymond Carver short story.

51   Online Perfume & Cosmetic Sales in the US - Market Size 2002–2026, IBISWorld: https://www.ibisworld.com/industry-statistics/market-size/online-perfume-cosmetic-sales-united-states/

CHAPTER 11: YOUTH

52   "Nouvelle jeunesse pour Fragrance Resources," Cosmétique Magazine, Oct. 1, 2007.

53   Free Agent After a Highly Public Breakup with Creed, Marketer Laurice Rahme is Back in the Driver's Seat with Her Latest Venture, Bond No. 9," Beauty Biz, May 1, 2005.

54   "What Wounded Soldier Doesn't Want to Smell Zesty?" Gawker, May 25, 2006.

55   "Growing Creed in U.S." Women's Wear Daily, Dec. 10, 2010.

CHAPTER 12: THE STUDENT

56   The following story of Herault's entry into the bizarro Creed world comes from my interview of him.

CHAPTER 13: THE MASTERPIECE

57   "Creed," Women's Wear Daily, Aug. 27, 2010.

58   "Creed Expands Women's Offerings With New Scent and Digital Strategy," Women's Wear Daily, Aug. 7, 2018.

59   "ÇaFleureBon Young Perfumers: Julien Rasquinet of IFF + Naomi Goodsir Parfums

Draw," https://www.cafleurebon.com/cafleurebon-young-perfumers-julien-ras
quinet-of-iff-naomi-goodsir-parfums-draw/, Jan. 20, 2016.

60   ÇaFleureBon Young Perfumers: Julien Rasquinet of IFF + Naomi Goodsir Parfums
Draw," https://www.cafleurebon.com/cafleurebon-young-perfumers-julien-ras
quinet-of-iff-naomi-goodsir-parfums-draw/, Jan. 20, 2016.

61   At Roure, for instance, beginning in 1969, perfumer Raymond Chaillan was *chargé
des reprises* for a long list of famous scents he did not create himself originally:
Monsieur de Rauch, Monsieur de Givenchy, Coeur Joie, Givenchy lll, and Nina
Ricci Bigarade.

But what sort of work did that French phrase – which, translated literally, means
"in charge of recoveries" – entail back then? It could not mean Chaillan had to
rejigger fragrances to eliminate newly-banned ingredients – there were none –
science had yet to discover what harm certain chemicals could do. The big study
on the neurotoxicity of musk ambrette, for instance, was not conducted until 1984.

No, Chaillan had to adjust these fragrances if, beginning to founder on the
market, they were decided by the companies that had commissioned them to be
too artistically challenging for the public – insufficiently commercial – and that
opinion was made known to the company that had created them, Roure.

It made no difference which brilliant perfumer had first put the scent together;
it was simply Chaillan who had to make the work more generally appealing –
whatever that meant – once the client complaint was registered.

Times have changed, to a degree. All the fine fragrance folks at Givaudan are
aware of Clare Finn, a perfumer whose entire job is to alter fragrances per revised
ingredient guidelines (non-biodegradable materials are already being discarded,
those that induce photo-sensitivity have been phased out; and there's also the
constant issue of commodity scarcity and cost – how to keep a fragrance on the
market when a key element is no longer affordable or even available?).

And Pierre's old Roure colleague Jean-Louis Sieuzac was invited back to the
firm (by then already called Givaudan) to adjust the original YSL Opium alongside
a present-day Givaudan perfumer, Antoine Maisondieu.

62   The Nazi in charge of this salary withholding writes to the French collaborator: "I
would like to draw your attention to the fact that due to the Enemy Ordinance, no
dividends, royalties or other payments may be made to the hostile shareholders or
their agents.

"All remuneration due to the enemies is to be paid into the account of the 'Trustee
and auditor in the area of the military commander in France' at the Barclays Bank,
35, rue du 4 Septembre, in their favor.

CHAPTER 14: REVOLUTION

63   "France vs. U.S.: War of the Noses," The New York Times, Aug. 5, 1979.

64   A far more humorous and tragic father-son story – one that perhaps feels more relatable and real than Olivier and Erwin's but in fact is not: Rich or poor, mutually supportive or not, fathers and sons are – to be tautological and Turgenev-title-esque – always fathers and sons.

They want for their kids contentment and happiness, in the best of cases, but have difficulty setting aside their own ideas about how that's to be achieved. Biology plays its role. The sons are indeed destined to inherit at least some of the father's traits, including the vices for which every paterfamilias later tries to repent but cannot. It feels the time has come and gone. Harry Chapin knew always the time comes and goes. Can the present ever really be received?

Symrise perfumer Dave Apel:

David Apel: "My father, he would do anything, so there was a restaurant he worked with in Oakland, New Jersey, called the Hanson House which is no longer there, and he was the chef at the Hanson House and they had a problem with rats.

"So they got a rat guy in who would seal off all the rat holes except one and send a ferret in after the rats, but that was a disaster because the ferrets just killed the rats in the walls and they stunk.

"So one night my father, and this is the truth and it's insane, but it is true, he went in after the restaurant closed, he stayed there, he set himself up in the middle of the big butcher block preparing table in the middle of the kitchen, surrounded himself by number 10 cans, which are the great big cans that you used for all kinds of produce in a restaurant, with his bow and arrow.

"And we grew up hunting and fishing. I grew up in the woods, and he was there to shoot rats, and he was terrified because he hated rats. So—

Me: "Wait, sorry, how does the can and the bow and arrow work together?"

Apel: "He wanted to put it around himself as a little fortress. And he was in the room waiting for those rats to come out, and when he saw a rat, he would shoot at it with the bow and arrow...and he shot at one, and the arrow ricocheted off of everything and splintered and knocked all the cans down. So those are kind of typical restaurant stories."

Me: "No, that's not a typical...how is that typical?"

"That's typical, yeah."

CHAPTER 15: DU CÔTÉ DE CHEZ BOURDON, OR, PIERRE'S WAY

65   As Simone and Sartre rented their rooms, I wonder whether they ever needed the superintendent at an odd hour of the night, but unable to reach him, set to work on the plumbing themselves with unfortunate but humorous consequence.

Actually, the Hotel Mistral, having gone all in on this historical connection, has placed two tiles in my bathroom featuring illustrations of the thinkers. Simone makes me nervous about disrobing. I'm neither a believer in the paranormal nor a prude, but my junk being just as wrinkly and unspectacular as the term implies, I worry just how insignificant it might to seem in the existential scheme of things. Bash me for a heteronormative outlook, but I just don't seem to mind that this same reproductive pouch might add to Sartre's "Nausea." Let him deal with it.

66   "The Make-Over at Estee Lauder," The New York Times Magazine, Nov. 29, 1987.

67   **"Don't turn a blind eye; Removing That Waterproof Mascara Does Not Have to Be a Painful or Painstaking Experience," Daily Mail (London), Sept. 29, 1994.**

68   **"Vive le visagiste," The Irish Times, March 31, 1997.**

69   **"It's the nose that knows," The Herald (Glasgow), Aug. 15, 1998.**

70   I choose this spelling for "Repellin" because it's the version found in French court documents, despite the name being elsewhere spelled "Reppelin."

71   For a further look at the brand shift from Repellin to Durrani: https://marques.ex pert/repellin-pierre-louis/pierre-durrani-dd-design-by-pierre-durra-99789754 .html#

For the appeals court ruling on Repellin's legal case: https://webcache.googleuser content.com/search?q=cache:p_OCXHs4zKkJ:https://www.doctrine.fr/d/CA/Pa ris/2002/INPIM20020175+&cd=1&hl=en&ct=clnk&gl=us

72   Much of the following is Atmeh's account to me.

73   "Perfume and Politics," The New Yorker, May 3, 1930. (See: https://www.newyor ker.com/magazine/1930/05/03/perfume-and-politics)

74   Call me Deacon Blues.

About the Author

Gabe Oppenheim is also the author of "Boxing in Philadelphia," an account of the fighters, past and present, of that gritty city — and many periodical pieces besides. Plus some fiction and a few screenplays. He lives in Manhattan in an old hotel whose former dumbwaiter openings have been converted into bookshelf nooks (his own now doubling as a display case for some of the gaudier perfume bottles in an ever-expanding collection).